Sweet
Promised
Land

BOOKS BY ROBERT LAXALT

Violent Land: Tales the Old Timers Tell

Sweet Promised Land

A Man in the Wheatfield

Nevada

In A Hundred Graves: A Basque Portrait

Nevada: A History

A Cup of Tea in Pamplona

Sweet Promised Land

by ROBERT LAXALT

Illustration by George Carlson

Foreword by William A. Douglass

UNIVERSITY OF NEVADA PRESS
RENO AND LAS VEGAS

BASQUE SERIES EDITOR: WILLIAM A. DOUGLASS

The paper used in this book meets the requirements
of American National Standard for Information
Sciences—Permanence of Paper for Printed Library
Materials, ANSI Z39.48-1984. Binding materials
were chosen for strength and durability.
(∞)

Library of Congress Cataloging-in-Publication Data

Laxalt, Robert, 1923–
  Sweet promised land.

  (Basque series)
  Reprint. Originally published: New York: Harper, c1957.
  Summary: The account a son writes of his father, an old Basque sheep-
herder who lived and worked in the American West for most of his life, who,
in fulfilling his dream of returning to the Pyrenees, came to a new realization
of what America meant to him.
  1. Laxalt, Dominique. 2. Basque Americans—Biography. 3. Laxalt,
Robert, 1923–   —Family. [1. Laxalt, Dominique. 2. Basques—United
States]
I. Carlson, George, 1940–   ill. II. Title. III. Series.
E184.B14L3   1986   979.3'049992024 [B] [92]   86-13204
ISBN 0-87417-114-8 (alk. paper)
ISBN 0-87417-118-0 (lim. ed. : alk. paper)

University of Nevada Press, Reno, Nevada 89557 USA
Copyright © Robert Laxalt 1957. All Rights Reserved
Printed in the United States of America
ISBN 0-87417-114-8 (trade edition)
ISBN 0-87417-118-0 (limited edition)

For Mom
Urrun bizi naiz, bainan bihotzez bethi zuekin.

Foreword

Robert Laxalt's *Sweet Promised Land* is a classic. The word "classic" is frequently abused, particularly when referring to recent literary works, but *Sweet Promised Land* qualifies because it is both innovative in concept and influential in its impact.

First published by Harper and Row in 1957, the book describes the journey that the author's father made to his European homeland after half a century as an immigrant Basque sheepman in the American West. The trip serves as the catalyst for Dominique's reminiscences about his childhood in the Basque Country and his struggle on the American frontier, and it is only by fulfilling his dream of visiting his birthplace that he comes to the realization that America has become his true home.

The book received high critical acclaim and became the first selection of the National Book Society in England and an alternate of the Literary Guild in the

United States. It was also published in translation in both Germany and France. *Sweet Promised Land*, then, heralded the arrival of a promising new American writer. However, it quickly became more than a simple literary triumph, a successful first book. In order to appreciate why this was the case it is necessary to place the work in several contexts.

In retrospect it is clear that by the late 1950s America was about to undergo a major reexamination of the common assumptions underpinning the national consensus. As the nation came of age during the late nineteenth and early twentieth centuries it had pursued a relentless "melting pot" policy that was designed to assimilate the massive influx of immigrants who might otherwise pose a threat to the country's mainstream British and colonial heritage. The new Americans might be encouraged to contribute a dish or two to the eclectic national cuisine, and they could pretty much count upon tolerance for their religious inclinations, but the remainder of their cultural distinctiveness was deemed unacceptable. Persons who clung to their native language and who continued to manifest Old World lifeways were suspect.

However, the cumulative effects of two world wars, the Great Depression, and increasingly restrictive U.S. immigration legislation meant that by the 1950s nearly half a century had transpired since America's gates had opened wide to the world's (or at least to Europe's) "huddled masses." As the numbers of new immigrants dwindled and the ethnic neighborhoods aged and withered, it was time for second thoughts. What had we lost in demanding that our forefathers renounce their ethnic essence in order to become Americans?

If the nation's population of European descent was ripe for nostalgia, its non-white minorities were poised on the brink of rebellion. For this was the eve of the civil rights movement that was about to galvanize Blacks, Hispanics, Asians, and American Indians into a potent lobby for social reform. A renewal of ethnic pride was a critical ingredient in the transformation, a pride that could only be ratified through a new understanding of each group's worth and past contributions to American culture.

Another factor in the equation of the late 1950s deserves mention. Developments within the American economy during the first half of the twentieth century prompted massive internal migration between regions and from the countryside to the cities. An urban job and suburban home far from the familiar relatives and neighborhoods of one's childhood were the epitome of success in the new consumer society. However, the life-style took its psychological toll as rootlessness gradually became restlessness. Materialism was not an entirely satisfactory reward for the obvious decline in religious, family, and community values. Furthermore, some Americans were beginning to weary of the nation's new superpower status in world affairs. The euphoria of the victory in World War II dissipated in the Korean stale-mate and the general chill of the cold war confrontation. The late 1950s, then, was a precursor of the counterculture movement in America, a quest for a simpler life-style and purpose.

Such were the times when Robert Laxalt set pen to paper to relate his father's story. If hindsight tells us that the moment was propitious for a simple tale of one immigrant's struggle against formidable odds in the mountains and deserts of the American West, and his ultimate recognition of the basic values that made America indeed the sweet promised land, that fact was by no means evident to Robert or his contemporaries. Subsequently, both the "roots" phenomenon and the counterculture movements would culminate in vigorous and prolific genres within American letters, but neither existed at the time that Laxalt crafted his work. William Saroyan was the only writer to whom the critics managed to liken the author of *Sweet Promised Land,* and even then the obvious stylistic differences made the comparisons tenuous at best. It was only later that Laxalt read the California novelist. Saroyan said in a letter to Harper and Row, "*Sweet Promised Land* really delighted and moved me—the anger (rage) of the old man at the cougar (mountain lion) is magnificent, unforgettable, profoundly meaningful—about the relationship between righteousness and risk." The western writer Tom Lea provided another testimonial when he wrote, "The power of *Sweet Promised Land* has stayed with me. I have reread it more than once. I have been an advocate, admirer and frequent mentioner of that book's qualities since its publication." *Sweet Promised Land,* then, was very much an American original as well as a harbinger of things to come.

In reviewing the book one critic noted, "Laxalt speaks not only for the Basques but for the Italians and Yugoslavs, for the Swedes and the Irish, the Portuguese and the Greeks—all our second generation citizens. Rarely have they had a more eloquent spokesman." Nonetheless, the message was particularly important for Basque-Americans. Descendants of a homeland divided between Spain and France, Basques lacked the ready recognition of a nationality with a country delineated on the world map and with a seat in the United Nations. The Basque-Americans were few in number, scattered lightly over the vastness of the American West, and most were engaged in sheep husbandry under open-range conditions. This occupational specialization meant that they were, for the most part, far removed from the day-to-day scrutiny of their neighbors. Indeed, to the extent that Basques entered the common awareness it was usually in a negative fashion. Their ethnic success as sheepherders *par excellence* identified them closely with the region's most denigrated occupation. Basque-Americans had learned the hard way to limit expressions of their heritage to the privacy of the home or the semiprivate context of the Basque hotels found in towns of the sheep-raising districts.

Sweet Promised Land provided the Basque-Americans with their own literary spokesman. Dominique's story encapsulated a little bit of the struggle experienced by most Basque-American families, and Robert Laxalt's simple eloquence in narrating it captured the imagination of the wider public. In a sense, for Basque-Americans the book's success legitimated their own ethnic sentiments—even to themselves. Laxalt received poignant letters from Basques throughout the American West thanking him for reinforcing their pride in their heritage. Within two years after publication of the book the interest it stimulated prompted an attempt to organize a National Basque Festival in Sparks, Nevada. Laxalt became one of the organizers, and his fan mail provided the network of contacts that the committee used to publicize the event throughout the Basque community of the region. Several thousand persons attended, and the Sparks celebration became the stimulus and prototype of the popular Basque festivals that are currently held each summer in several communities of the American West.

If *Sweet Promised Land* provided Basque-Americans with a source of ethnic pride it had a similar effect for the rest of Laxalt's fellow Nevadans. Residents of a state that was known for its legalized gaming, prostitution, and quick divorces, Nevadans were accustomed to negative coverage in the national media. In the 1950s they were smarting from the state's mobster image as depicted in the Kefauver Report. *Sweet Promised Land* provided a welcome relief from the imagery of easy money and a sleazy life style. It was a simple morality play set amidst soaring mountain ranges and searing deserts far removed from the gambling glitter. It depicted a simple man with sound basic values disposed to confront adversity while sacrificing his youth to gain a foothold for his family in the America that he loved. For Nevadans, *Sweet Promised Land* became *their* book. It was an antidote for lurid depictions of the state, and one could read it for personal reassurance and then send it to friends and relatives out of state as a way of saying "I do not live in Sodom and Gomorrah."

One of the effects of *Sweet Promised Land* was to provide considerable recognition for the Laxalt family. Robert's older brother Paul was an attorney by profession who had served in the early 1950s as district attorney for Carson City before going into private practice. In 1962 Paul ran successfully as a Republican for lieutenant governor of Nevada. In 1964 he was narrowly defeated in the United States Senate race by Democratic incumbent Howard Cannon. In 1966, when Paul was a candidate for the governorship, his campaign committee purchased several hundred copies of *Sweet Promised Land* for distribution in Clark County (southern Nevada), a Democratic bastion and an area where he lacked name recognition. He won the election. In 1974 Paul contested a United States Senate seat against Democrat Harry Reid. Republicans were in the minority in the state, and a Democratic landslide seemed inevitable in the immediate aftermath of the Watergate scandal. Robert was active in his brother's campaign and deeply committed to his election. He was also disturbed by aspersions cast upon the Laxalt family in the heat of battle. He therefore agreed to write an epilogue for a special paperback edition of *Sweet Promised Land,* detailing Paul's career. The press run of 30,000 copies was distributed by the campaign committee throughout the state, and Paul won the election by 624 votes.

Paul is currently finishing his second term in the United States Senate. He has been extraordinarily successful, serving as President Reagan's campaign manager, confidante, and friend, as well as chairing the Republican National Committee. At this writing he is receiving serious mention as the possible Republican candidate for the presidency in 1988.

The success of *Sweet Promised Land* also helped Robert to realize some of his own goals and to facilitate those of others. When he wrote the book Laxalt was director of the Publications and News Service at the University of Nevada. His abiding interest in the history of Nevada and the region prompted him to propose creation of a university press. It was a bold idea for a small state university. However, Laxalt's new visibility, and the positive impact of *Sweet Promised Land* on Nevadans in general, lent credibility to the project. At the time the balance of power in the state was held by the rural counties, and their legislators were particularly moved by the book. Laxalt's lobbying efforts in the Nevada State Legislature were successful, and in 1961 the University of Nevada Press was established.

That same year a group of consultants came to Reno to advise the university regarding the possible creation and mission of a research institute. Among their many suggestions was the one that the new Desert Research Institute might consider focusing upon the Basques of the American West and Europe as one of its interests. No other American university had done so to date and the Basque culture and language posed a whole range of research possibilities. Again, the interest aroused by *Sweet Promised Land* stimulated a new initiative, and who was more appropriate to launch it than its author? Laxalt was asked to coordinate the effort but declined on the grounds that he was not a scholar in the strict sense of the word. He did, however, agree to help lay the groundwork until someone could be found. He had already planned a sabbatical leave year in the Basque Country in order to write a book about it. He agreed to prepare a Basque bibliography as a consultant to both the Library of Congress and the Desert Research Institute. Because of Laxalt the noted French Basque Studies specialist Phillippe Veyrin, who was terminally ill at the time, decided that his personal library should

xvi

be offered to the University of Nevada upon his death. The Veyrin collection became the basis for what has ultimately become one of the world's major Basque libraries.

In 1967 the Basque Studies Program was launched officially by the Desert Research Institute. Throughout the past twenty years Robert Laxalt has remained one of its staunchest supporters, participants, and advisers. He was particularly instrumental in the creation of the Basque Book Series within the University of Nevada Press. His devotion to its success is reflected in the fact that he has submitted his two subsequent Basque books to it. *In a Hundred Graves: A Basque Portrait* and *A Cup of Tea in Pamplona* both received high critical acclaim and have been mainstays for the University of Nevada Press. From a simple sales standpoint the books might have done better had they been published by a commercial house. However, this was not an issue since Robert Laxalt chose to donate the royalties from *Hundred Graves* to the Basque Book Series anyway. It therefore seems particularly appropriate that the book that facilitated creation of the University of Nevada Press should now be published by it.

Such was the impact of *Sweet Promised Land.* The book may be said to have helped launch a literary genre, a people's pride, a region's ethnic festival, a state's image, an illustrious political career, a university press, and a unique studies program. Would any or all of these developments have happened without the book? Possibly. But of course we can never know—for *Sweet Promised Land* became inextricably intertwined with the very processes that it influenced.

Finally, for the past twenty years it has been my pleasure and privilege to know Robert Laxalt as a fine colleague and friend. I have therefore been privy to many of his personal recollections. As I contemplated writing this foreword I decided that it was worth telling some of the "story behind the story."

By the late 1950s Robert Laxalt had been a journalist and wire service correspondent. That he also possessed literary flair was evident in the fact that he had published many articles in national magazines. Indeed, when Robert decided to go along on his father's return trip to the Basque Country he proposed writing a story about it for the *Saturday Evening Post*. The editors were intrigued but urged him to consider a book-length treatment instead.

Robert therefore took copious notes throughout the journey. For a year after his return he made several false starts on the manuscript. Several factors were at work. He had never undertaken a book before and therefore experienced the natural self-doubts of the aspiring novelist. A colleague had suggested to him that he should take an epic approach to the Basque-American experience in the American West, and so he struggled to universalize the details of one man's journey so they would represent the odyssey of a whole people's emigration to America. Not surprisingly, the approach led him into one blind alley after another. Finally, he secluded himself for the proverbial one last try. In the midst of his frustration he rather absentmindedly wrote the first line of *Sweet Promised Land*—"My father was a sheepherder, and his home was the hills." The simplicity of the statement provided the needed focus, liberating him from the straitjacket of overstylization.

The story flowed easily from there, as Robert began to write for his own satisfaction and edification. The more personal it became the more convinced he was that it would be of little interest to others. He was therefore surprised when Harper and Row offered him a contract after reviewing the first four chapters. At the same time he experienced a sense of panic. The book was clearly an invasion of his family's privacy. It also represented a very personal statement of a son's love and respect for a father whom he scarcely knew prior to their shared journey. For Dominique had always been a distant figure, physically removed from the family circle for months at a time and aloofly patriarchal in his Old World ways. The journey had provided father and son with the first real opportunity to share something together; the book had the potential of compromising this precious intimacy, or even of making it maudlin. Laxalt was also fearful that he would fail to do justice to the reality of the Basque Country that he had come to know and love for the first time. For if the trip back represented a release for the father, it had ensnared the son. He was determined to return and penetrate more deeply into the fascinating Old World Basque traditions. His commitment to learning more about a heritage that was his own, after all, made him question whether he was prepared as yet to make statements about it. It was therefore with considerable ambivalence that Robert completed the book, telling himself that the publishers would likely change their minds when they saw the whole manuscript.

Such was not the case and when Robert was faced with the final galley proofs he still had not told his father about the book. Dominique was on the summer sheep range in the Sierra Nevada above Carson City and the issue could no longer be avoided. Dominique was due to return to town and Robert volunteered to drive up to get him. He did so with considerable trepidation. That evening as the two men sat by the campfire Robert was about to broach the subject when he noticed the 30-30 carbine lying next to his father. Robert kept his silence.

The next morning he locked the rifle in the trunk of the car and they started the drive down to Carson City. Their progress was slowed by roadwork. Finally Robert turned to Dominique and said, "Pop, you know that trip we took to Europe?"

"Yeah."

"Well, I wrote a book about it."

Dominique was silent for a few moments and then said, "When do you think they're going to finish this road?"

WILLIAM A. DOUGLASS
Coordinator
Basque Studies Program

August 1986

Sweet
Promised
Land

My father was a sheepherder, and his home was the hills. So it began when he was a boy in the misted Pyrenees of France, and so it was to be for the most of his lifetime in the lonely Sierra of Nevada. And seeing him in a moment's pause on some high ridge, with the wind tearing at his wild thickness of iron-gray hair and flattening his clothes to his lean frame, you could understand why this was what he was meant to be.

My mother used to say a man like that should never get married, because he didn't go with a house. And in her own way, I guess she was right, because I could remember thinking it and knowing it too when I saw him bent over a campfire at night, with the light playing against the deep bronze of his features and making dark hollows of his eyes, and with its own humor, etching more strongly a nose a little off kilter from where he'd been kicked in the face during his horsebreaking days.

I believe that if there had been a hundred sheep camps in the hills, I could have known my father's in an instant. In that little circle of canvas and leather, things had as much their own place as in a living room.

If it was a new camp and not an old stop, he laid the fire pit to his precise liking, in a sheltered half cave of rocks faced against the afternoon wind, so that there would be as few ashes as possible in the evening meal. His cayaks or pack bags were always stacked to the left of the tent flap, covered by a square of canvas, and held down with a shovel or a carbine. Summer or winter, his canvas bed and mattress of boughs or branches was placed inside the tent with its head near the entrance, so that if it were winter and there was a little tin stove inside, he could reach over and start his morning fire without getting out of bed.

When I was a boy, and we brothers would visit him each summer for a few weeks, I wondered about his neatness in the camps. It seemed to me that the mountains were a good place to shuck off the most of manners and cleanliness. And then, finally, I came to realize that the sheep camp was my father's house.

In all the time that we were growing up, I can remember my father's presence in our white frame home in Carson City only in rare and fleeting visits. The sprawling rooms and old-fashioned high ceilings were as much of a mystery to him as any other cluster of four walls. Except for the wedding portrait in its gold frame or the one suit hung far back in the bedroom closet, the house carried little hint of a father's existence.

The garage, however, was a different matter. From ceiling to floor and flush with the front, it was filled with the chronicle of my father's life since he had come to this country. In that mountain of leather and canvas and old pelts, you could find hair chaps from when he was a horsebreaker, a cartridge belt from the early time of trouble with the cattlemen, an old packsaddle with the wood polished and worn that he put away when his Jenny died, and, sometimes, a brand-new sheep hook or braided rawhide reins, because so often when he bought something new he would put it in the garage to save it, and then forget he bought it.

There's a bearing and a cast of face that come with men who lived in that American day when the ranges were open and the western streets were dirt. You can see it in the old-timers who come to the big rodeos in Reno, and fewer of them each year, who carry themselves as straight as if they were still in the saddle, with the quiet dignity and privacy in their faces that come from much time spent alone, and they are not unlike the faces of old Indian chiefs.

These were the men of leather and bronze who had been rich as barons one day and broke and working for wages the next, who had ridden big and powerful horses, and who had met in the lonely desert and talked a while, hunkering over a sagebrush fire and a blackened coffeepot, and, even though they had battled with life, they had learned to accept it, because they had learned first to bow their heads to the winter blizzards and the desert sun. And my father was one of them.

In him, such opposites as gentleness and violence in the same nature wore like a glove. It was exactly what you would expect of a man like that.

I can remember one spring when a late blizzard hit our lambing corrals in the desert. There were only a few roofed sheds, not nearly enough to cover a few thousand ewes having their lambs at all hours of the day or night. The lambs were born in open corrals whipped and soaked with sleeting snow. We could do nothing else but drag them with sheep hooks to the flimsy protection of a corral fence, and hope they lived until the storm passed and the sun came out.

Of course, it was impossible that they could. In the days and nights that the storm held, we lost nearly every lamb that was born.

And yet, in this time of screaming winds and wetness and death, my father came into the cabin one night soaked to the skin and stumbling tired. His heavy sheepskin coat was wrapped around a bundle in his arms, and in the bundle were two new lambs. The ewe had died in birth, and the lambs were motherless.

The dinner of scrambled eggs and pork that I had put together went ignored on the table. My father put the lambs in the corner by the stove, where they steamed and shivered, and for the first time mewed hopefully with the warmth. My father heated goat's milk in a pan and knelt in the corner, feeding them a teaspoonful at a time. When he was done and the lambs were asleep, he stood up and weaved past the table and the cold dinner without a word, and fell into his bunk.

On the other side of nature's fence, however, things were a little different. In the rare times that my father got mad, there was no middle ground. He did not waste any time talking. He just went after his rifle.

Perhaps this disconcerting attitude toward arguments harked back to the early days of trouble with cattlemen, but at any rate it caused my mother no end of gray hairs. Once, when my father was home, someone men-

4

tioned to him what a former sheepman in the next county had said: that my father didn't "give a damn about his family," else he would sell his sheep and come home.

Upon inspection, the remark was a righteous one born out of the sheepman's resentment against having to live in town. But my father was raised in a time when insults were insults. Two minutes after he had heard the remark, he and his rifle were out the door and on the highway. It took a flurry of phone calls, armed men, and frantic apologies to avert bloodshed.

Another time, something happened that I have never really been able to understand. At first, it made me more angry with my father than anything else. But afterward, I remembered other things, such as the times he had approached wild stallions fighting in the hills, and even though they knew he was there they had ignored him and gone on fighting as if no stranger were there at all. Finally, I came to understand part of it, but, being more town-bred than not, I will never be able to see the whole of it.

That summer, my father was ranging the sheep in the Sierra foothills. It was country where the meadows ran for miles through the forests, and so the sheep could feed for weeks in that one range.

The first time I went to visit him, he mentioned that a pair of mountain lions had been bothering the sheep. He had cut their tracks a number of times, and on two different nights in his camp had heard them coughing from the canyon. His dog, Barbo, made furious nightly forays into the trees, but of course he was careful not to get within fighting distance.

5

The lions must have been killing elsewhere, because they had not as yet taken any of the lambs. Still, they were working up to it, and the time would not be long. My father did not have a carbine in the camp with him, so I said that I would bring one the next time I came. He shrugged and said, "It won't do no good. When it happens, they'll be durned sure I'm not looking."

It was a few weeks before I could make another trip to the camp, and when I did it was with the right carbine and the wrong cartridges. By the time I discovered my mistake, I was already in the hills and too far from home to turn back.

When I reached the camp, I learned that the lions had already hit the band. It had been a quiet kill, and my father had no knowledge of it until he noticed a ewe bleating lonely and searching for her lamb. Then he backtracked to the bed ground of the night before and found the splash of blood that marked the slaughter.

He must have been mad at the time, because when he told me about it there was still heat in his eyes. I felt a new twinge of conscience about my mixup with the carbine and cartridges, but he didn't seem to mind. In spite of his anger, he was a little bit philosophical. Now that the lions had made their kill, he felt he would be left alone until the sheep had moved from the meadow country.

It was late afternoon and the shadows long when I started the walk to my car. My father came down the hill with me, on his way to gathering the band. There was an evening breeze coming up, and it was in our faces, and it brought with it the occasional tinkle of a bell. Every once in a while, as we cut down through the ravines, we could catch glimpses of the sheep scattered in the meadow below.

Then, almost inaudibly, the breeze brought to us the low sound of running hoofs. My father stopped and peered down into the meadow. Abruptly, he changed our direction and began to walk to the right of the hill in front of us. At his heels, Barbo started to whimper, but my father silenced him with a quick command. I wanted to ask him what he had seen, but, for some reason, I had the feeling it was none of my business.

To one side of the hill in front of us, there was a narrow ravine that emptied into the meadow below. My father swung into it with his long stride, and I followed, trying to make as little sound as possible. We descended rapidly, and in a few minutes we were almost out of the ravine. My father was about twenty feet in front of me when he reached the meadow, and came face to face with the lion.

I had been looking at the ground, and the first warning I had of it was when I heard the sob in Barbo's throat. I jerked my head up and saw the lion. I remember only feeling an odd shock at the fact of his freedom, and then my mind and my face both froze.

They must have stared at each other for full seconds. The lion cocked his head to one side, almost curiously, and rumbled once deep in his chest. Then, slowly, my father raised his *makila*, his walking stick, and began to advance toward the lion. The rumble started again, this time in ominous warning, and with that startling suddenness of motion the lion dropped into a crouch.

Even then, there was not a hint of hesitation in my

7

father's movements. He did not falter once in his stride. His stick was still raised in the air, as though not to fend but strike, and his pose was menacing. They were only a few feet apart when the lion, as though he had suddenly become uncertain, straightened and then crouched again, and then incredibly began to back up. And now, his neck was not rigid any more. He tossed his head, snarling and showing his fangs. And still my father pursued him in that relentless advance.

When I remember, I realize that the lion must not even have known where he was backing, because when his hindquarters met the pole fence he recoiled as if he had been burned, and in one lightning motion wheeled completely around. And when he turned to face my father again, the confusion was gone and the motion deadly. This time, his eyes were burning red and he was crouching to spring. And still my father did not pause an instant, but came toward him with his stick raised in the air.

There was a single beat of time before the lion sprang when he seemed to arrest his muscles and reset them. Afterward I could remember, but at the instant I could not understand that this had happened. When the lion left the ground, my mind had already prepared its next image, that of seeing my father go down in a blinding flurry of talons. But he did not. By some feat, the lion seemed to leap directly at him, and then arch his body away so that he actually came to light at the side of my father.

And then, almost in the same motion, he began to run away. He did not bolt, but took his leave loping un-hurriedly in the direction of the trees, looking back and

8

snarling every once in a while, as though maintaining a degree of self-respect. My father did not follow him, but stood now with his stick to the ground and leaning on it a little, watching until the lion had disappeared in the trees.

When it was over, I felt hot words at my lips. But then my father turned and there was a private pity in his face that had not yet fully vanished, as though now he felt sorrow at the lion's shame, and I could not say a word, because I knew then that foolhardiness had been no part of it at all.

ananananananananananananananan *2*

My father had married my mother when he was rich in sheep. She was Basque too, although raised more gently than my father in the soft lowlands of the French Pyrenees.

Both out of necessity and background, she was a practical woman. Her family had a small hotel and a travel agency in Bordeaux, and she had learned business there, and once she had even gone to cooking school in Paris. She came to America only to see her brother, who had been a French soldier and who was dying from the poison gas he had breathed in the war. But, once here, she had loved America and its ways immediately, and never showed a desire to return to France.

She met and married my father in Reno, and after he had gone broke in sheep and she had had to bear her children in rough camps and ghosted little towns, she had taken what little money they had and bought into a small hotel in Carson City. Later, as they prospered and my father went back into the hills with his own sheep, she had bought other business properties and the house in which we were to pass the rest of our childhood.

After that, I think our family spent half of its growing-up life looking for my father. We looked for him so much when we all lived at home that I used to dream about it. But this dream did not stem from fancy. It had its roots deep in reality, and it went something like this:

My brothers and I, Paul the older and John and Mick the younger, would be relaxing in the big dining room of our house in Carson City when my mother would come into the room in a high state of excitement. Either there were some business papers that needed my father's signature, or one of our two sisters, Suzanne or Marie, would be sick.

"We have to find your father," my mother would say.

My brothers and I would regard her in various postures of silence, but there was an awakening of something in our eyes.

"Go find him," my mother would say, a little irritated that we had not taken it up of our own free will.

"Oh sure," John would say. "Go find him."

Paul, who was the big brother, would be more constructive. "We don't know where he is." And Mick would add, "We haven't seen him in two months."

My mother would make a fluttering sweep of her hand, a gesture that covered an even one hundred miles of desert and Sierra Nevada. "He's in the hills," she would say easily.

"Oh sure," John, who had become a cynic at a very early age, would say. "He's in the hills."

"That's right," my mother would affirm with the finality of one whose word was law. "Go find him."

Then she would leave the room, and we would stare at each other in mute and hopeless contemplation of one thousand lost canyons of desert and mountains. The dream would end here, and it was just in time.

They say there are incidents in people's lives that chart their futures. Though all we brothers had them, and they were inexorably entwined with sheep, I think that John's incident was the most significant. It happened one time when he was looking for my father.

That summer, it was John's turn to tend camp. This meant that every week John would load up the old stake truck with grub for the sheep camp and go into the hills, there to meet my father at some appointed bend in a lost road. After several years of coping with his sons, Pop nearly always chose roads for the meeting places, so there would be no confusion. It was not a joking matter to be caught in the hills without food.

John had been faring well that summer. In spite of his modest protests, he was a good man with both livestock and mountains, as my father had often pointed out. He had kept every appointment faithfully, and there had been a minimum of searching for sheep track or shouting from high ground, where the echoes will carry into hidden canyons.

Then one day, when the sheep were in the foothills and somewhat hidden by the high sagebrush, John drove right past everything—the bend in the road, the sheep, and the camp. My father, who was resting on his canvas bed after lunch, saw him pass. As he said afterward, he would have shouted except that he thought John was going up the road to find a place wide enough to turn around.

But John kept on going. After about five miles, he came to the conclusion something had gone wrong, and got out of the truck to look for tracks. When he could not find any fresh ones, he decided that perhaps my father had not come down into the foothills after all. So he drove even higher.

My father held the sheep in check until midafternoon, scanning the hills for John's return. Then he could do nothing else but move. Pop was a sheepherder, and feed for the sheep came first, and his own, second.

It was dark by the time John came home to Carson City, dusty and discouraged, and with the grub still in the old truck. When he told the family what had happened, no one was especially worried. There had been missed connections before, and my father usually kept enough food aside to tide him over for a while. Since his sons had begun to tend camp, he had come to expect most anything in the sheep business.

When John failed to find my father on the next day, the family become a little concerned. But we still had faith in John, so the burden of finding my father rested on his shoulders alone. The rest of us were sympathetic listeners.

By the end of the third day, John was becoming frantic. He had literally walked a hundred miles, his eyes were red from searching for tracks, and he was hoarse from shouting. It was then that the family decided I should help, so I took off from my summer job in town for a day.

But one day didn't turn out to be long enough. By the time two more had passed, I was saddlesore, my father's two horses were so lame they could barely hobble to water, and John was at the point of exhaustion. Between us, it seemed we had covered every Sierra ridge this side of California. We missed one, however, and that was the one my father used to return to the high country.

The family dinner exactly one week from the day John drove past the bend in the road was a grim one. There was a drizzling rain outside that added to our depression. By now, there was talk of surrendering pride and asking another Basque sheepman to help. And I had even imposed upon a friend of mine, a former fighter pilot, to take me on an afternoon of hazard-fraught and fruitless passes at the mountains in a light plane. My father told us afterward he felt like taking a shot at some damned fool in an airplane who scared the sheep out of their wits one afternoon. I never said a word.

But as the family was eating dinner, there was a telephone call. It was the flume keeper at a mountain lake just over the rim of the high Sierra. He had been alerted about our predicament. Over the buzz of his single phone line, he said that late that afternoon he had seen what he thought was a band of sheep coming down from the mountain rim. And, just before dark, he had looked through his field glasses again and seen a fire on the other side of the lake. John didn't even wait to say good-by, but hung up the phone and dashed through the door.

He finally found my father that night and took him his grub. The last leg of the trip was at blackest night in a pitching motorboat, guided by the flume keeper across his rain-driven mountain lake. My father never said an irritated word to John, even though he had been living on bread crusts and goat's milk for three days, and, when his burro had run away with his bed, had spent one rainy night in a hollow log.

All this was too much for John. When he came home late that night, he was quiet and withdrawn. Like my older brother, he had decided to go to law school.

Some time later, when prices were good and when it became apparent to him that none of his sons would follow him in the livestock business, my father sold his sheep.

Afterward, he came home to the house in Carson City for his first prolonged stay. It was a rare reunion. The family was happy, because for a few years past everyone had been trying to convince my father that he should come home. As my mother told him, "You're not a young man any more, to go kicking around those hills like that." She said this with conviction, even though my father, then sixty-five years old, could still walk his sons down to their knees.

My father did not adjust very well to living in a house. He could not sit in any easy chair or sofa, but quietly preferred to relax on the floor or on a hard chair. And though he slept alone and on high in an attic room, the family could hear him tossing until late at night.

To keep busy, he chopped wood. At every pretext, he escaped to the mountains to haul down dead tree trunks and limbs, stacking them in the back yard for sawing and splitting. After a few months, the yard looked like a lumber mill, and there was firewood stacked neatly in every conceivable corner of the house. Everywhere we turned, there was firewood. Little rooms that we had forgotten existed were jammed with it, and in order to walk through the alley one had to thread one's way warily through towering avenues of firewood.

When the work possibilities in firewood were exhausted, my father built a corral, the likes of which I am certain has never been seen in Nevada. He built it in a sagebrush flat near town with the idea of using it at some vague time when he might go back into sheep, but it never held a head of stock. For lumber, he used boards and posts that once graced the old territorial hotel my folks had torn down to make way for new places of business. It was the sturdiest corral in the state, and also the fanciest. No other corral, I am sure, could claim an elaborate sprinkling of gingerbread trim and pillars that once were the pride of a hotel.

After that, my father began to pace. He had always managed to appear cramped in a house, but now he resembled something caged. His skin unbelievably lost its deep bronze, and, for the first time we could remember, he mentioned that he had a pain.

It was after dinner one night that my father picked up the evening newspaper. No matter how much light there was in the room, he always held his paper inches away from the glare of a lamp, force of habit from long years of reading in his tent at night by the dim light of a candle or a kerosene lantern. And, also, he was far-sighted from his life in the mountains, and so he held it at arm's length.

My father was reading in this fashion when he gave a start. He composed himself quickly and continued to read with an obvious intensity. When he was through, he folded the newspaper and put it down, and then went directly to his attic room. After a moment, the family began to hear sounds of rummaging and clumping. My brother picked up the paper and thumbed through it until he found the story. A Basque of involved and familiar name, who had sold his sheep and retired a few months before, had died.

The next day, in the early dawn before the family was awake, my father left the house. And, several days later, we learned that he had signed on as a herder for a big sheep outfit in the next valley. He had gone back to the mountains to stay.

So it was that we had passed into another generation and were still looking for him. By this time, the family was grown up, and I was married and living in nearby Reno and had a child of my own.

And, as ever when we went to look for him, it was a trying adventure. Since we had left Reno in the early morning, we had crossed valleys, passed through little Nevada communities that were even more quiet on Sunday, and taken wrong turns in the mountain roads.

When the car had stalled, we had gone searching for water in a canyon with a telltale flare of green willows, and carted it back in hats and cans. And, as ever, by the time we topped the last summit, it was late enough to be thinking of giving up the hunt and going home.

Then, unexpectedly, with the same surprise and elation that an explorer must feel, we saw what seemed to be the white and conical top of a tent, almost buried in the trees at the far end of a meadow.

Faintly, borne up and muted with the whir of the wind through the pines, came the sound of bells and bleating. It was a sheep camp. I filled my lungs and yelled, and in a little while my father answered. It came cupping down through the canyons in a call as old as the first Basque mountain man. It was my father's sheep camp.

Parking the car by the side of the road, we loaded ourselves with the newspapers and magazines and apple pie we had brought, and walked across the meadow to the tent. And buttoned in my shirt pocket was a letter from France that we knew bore news of my father's sister, who had suffered a stroke a month before.

Joyce, my wife, started a fire in the pit, and I went slowly up into the trees with our son Bruce to meet my father. There was dust in the upper canyon now, and the sounds were nearer. I listened for the dogs, so as to find out which way my father had turned the sheep, and then Bruce and I moved to one side so that we would not frighten the leaders when they came down.

It was a band of ewes and lambs, and the lambs, rambunctiously feeling their growth and pretending to be bosses of the situation, preceded the leaders over the ridge. Upon seeing us, they bucked and tossed their heels and tried to start a stampede of sorts. But the old leaders staidly ignored them and picked their way slowly down the slope, with no more than a passing glance at Bruce and me.

In a little while, my father appeared on the ridge. He stood there for a moment with the dogs at his heels, marking the way of the band, and then he sighted us below and waved with his *makila*. Bruce pulled loose

19

from my hand and went toddling up the hill to meet him. But my father's shaggy sheepdog greeted Bruce first and they both went down in a heap. Extricating Bruce from the tangle, my father lifted him in his arms. We cut away from the band and circled toward the camp. I think that was the first time I noticed that Pop was out of breath.

The first chill of evening was already in the air, and Joyce's fire was a welcome one. My father set about getting dinner—potatoes and lamb chops fried in the dutch oven. Spreading a square of clean canvas on the ground, he placed the *chahakoa,* the goatskin wine pouch, on it and broke out a huge new loaf of sourdough bread, scratching the sign of the cross on the back with his knife before he cut the first slice.

In my father's lifetime in the mountains, he had never seemed to know loneliness. He gave the appearance of being a quiet man, but he was not silent. He loved to talk, and his voice had a mountain softness to it that one never grew tired of hearing. Whether he met a lone hiker in the hills or on the street in town, he would stand and visit for hours. And whenever we came to see him in his camps, there would be a lively flow of conversation about everything from news of the family to affairs of the world.

But this time he was more quiet than usual. And as I watched him, I saw that there was a grayness about his mouth and eyes that had never been there before.

We sat cross-legged around the square of canvas and ate our dinner out of his tin plates. Once, Bruce escaped without our notice and ran behind the tent to where my father had tied down his other dog. It was a young and wild one who had not seen much of men, and who had shown his teeth at our approach. But, as wild dogs will, he stood in stiff and enduring agony as Bruce jerked playfully at his ears. After that, my father held Bruce on his lap and gave him the wineskin pouch to amuse himself.

He did not open the letter from the old country until we had finished dinner and were having bread and cheese and coffee. I think he expected the worst, because letters marked airmail from the old country always seemed to bear bad news. He still had four sisters living in the Basque country, and the one who had had the stroke was the oldest. Three brothers had come to America, and the only one living was my father, who was the youngest of the family.

As he read, his face showed no sign of whether the letter was good or bad. But midway through it, he stopped reading and said, "She's better." And in a moment, "They don't know how long she's going to last, but she's better."

Remembering the strokes that had taken speech away from my Uncle Pête, I asked, "Can she talk?"

He nodded. "She's in a good mind and they say she can still bring the words out good," he said. "But they don't hardly think she'll walk any more." And again, after a moment, "It's a shame."

"Was she pretty?" asked Joyce.

"Yes, she's pretty, and the liveliest thing," he said quickly, and then, remembering that it had been nearly fifty years since he had seen her, he shook his head as if to remind himself of this, and said, "But I guess she must be old by now." He touched his hand to his own gray hair. "I can't bring myself to think her hair is like this, but I guess it must be."

He began to reminisce. "It was in Bordeaux, the last time I seen her. She met me when I came down from the Pyrenees, and she put me on the train to Paris. I remember she bought me my first hat, and took away my beret for a remembrance. And at the station, when we said good-by, it was night and it was raining, and we watched the *carabiniers* ride by on their hosses. They had the uniforms with the gold and the shining steel helmets with the high plumes, and the animals they rode was proud."

And here we were again, as we had been so many times since we were young, at the moment when my father's thoughts turned again toward home. "Pop," I said, "why don't you think about going back for a visit?"

He shrugged. "They want me to," he said. "They wrote it again this time. She wants to see me awful bad."

Joyce and I looked at each other. How many times had the family been through this before? How many times had the desires and the dreams pyramided like this, and ended in nothing but conversation. We had repeated the arguments so many times that the words came almost from memory. But, as ever, I heard them coming from me again.

"There's no reason in the world you can't go," I said. "You don't have sheep any more. You don't have to work. You don't have any responsibilities, and," I added cautiously, "you'd better go while your health is still good."

This last seemed to have some effect. "That's right,"

he said with a puzzled look. "I guess it won't be forever." Then he thought a minute and shook his head in the old way, and said, "But it's so long a trip."

It wasn't that my father didn't understand about airplanes and the speed of modern travel. He understood it but could not realize it. When he had come to this country, he was only sixteen and did not know a word of English. And for someone who had never been twenty miles from home, the voyage across the ocean and the train trip over the broad expanse of the United States must have been endless and a little bit terrifying. He did not seem to be able to bridge the gap.

"It's not a long trip," said Joyce. "Say, for example, that you board the plane in San Francisco on Friday. Do you know that you could be in France on Saturday, and in the Pyrenees on Sunday? You could be having Sunday dinner with your family two days from the time you left."

His gaze grew distant at the thought of that, and then the frown crossed his brow. "But all the business about the passport and the shots. It takes a long time."

"But it doesn't," I protested. "You could have all that done while you were getting ready to go, buying clothes and things like that."

"Oh, I have a suit," he reminded us, as if we could forget the imperishable wedding suit that hung in the closet at home. "But I don't happen to have a suitcase."

"Pop," I said in exasperation, "there's more luggage in the family than you could ever use."

And so it went, with our arguments and his mild objections, growing weaker until he suddenly changed his tack and said, "Well, you know. I had a notion. If I was to leave in September, I could see the Marciano-LaStarza fight in New York on the way. They're going to fight at the Polo Grounds, you know."

When we burst into laughter, he looked at us perplexedly, as if he could not understand what had tickled us. I made my face serious again, and asked, "When will this job be through?"

"In just a few weeks," he said. "I'm taking the sheep down to the valley now. I will take maybe two weeks, and then I could get free if I wanted to."

He thought about it for a moment and was happier for it. And, as if to seal his own decision, he reached for the wine pouch. The conversation about the trip had ended on a happy note. But as we watched him raise the *chahakoa*, we knew in our minds that the trip would end right here. The dreams would be satisfied by talk, and by next week my father would convince himself of some pressing duty that would delay the trip until perhaps the next year, when we would talk about it again. And so it would go on as it had gone on for as far back as memory went.

I looked about the camp and saw the fire flickering dim in the open pit, and the dog with his shaggy head dozing in its fading warmth, the lonely tent in the trees, and my father's crude garb of the mountains, and all of us sitting on the bare ground, and beyond, the sky of the world outside, and the thought of gleaming planes and busy terminals and distant cities seemed to me overwhelming too, and I could begin to understand why it did end right here.

And then something happened that broke away the impossible. When my father raised the *chahakoa* and squeezed it, and the thin red stream of wine arched into his mouth, he choked and lowered it quickly.

"What's wrong?" I asked.

He turned his head away and coughed until his throat cleared. "I can't swallow so good," he said, touching his fingers to the side of his neck and pinching the skin as if it were numb.

"Something's gone wrong, hasn't it?"

He nodded, and the puzzled look came again into his eyes. "Last month," he said, "when it was so hot, and then the cold spell came, and up here there was snow and the wind turned to the north. It never happened to me before, even in the deserts, but the wind hurt me and I got so cold the water began to run from my ears." Then, as if remembering were not very far away, he hunched his shoulders. "I was a little way from the camp and I was bending over to get wood for the fire. And then I found myself lying on my back on the ground, and I didn't know how I got there. In my mind, I could hear the bells and the sheep, and I could see the mountains clear, but I couldn't move my body. I must of been there a long time, because when I opened my eyes again the sun was gone and the stars were out. I could move my body, but I couldn't stand up on my legs. I crawled to my bed and got in with my clothes on, and the next morning it was better and I wasn't suffering. But I couldn't swallow for a couple of days." He felt his chest and arms. "I got awful thin, and my body ain't back yet to what it was." He looked at us as if wanting an answer. "It must of been the cold, I guess," he asked more than said, and then added with a sad sort of sheepishness, "and maybe I'm getting to be an old man."

There was silence for a long time. Joyce pulled at a thread in her boot, and I made circles in the dirt with my knife. The fire crackled once as the flames ate into a pocket of pine, and the gas hissed away and died. Somewhere out in the darkness, a lone lamb called for his mother. "Well, maybe a little bit of both, Pop," I said, and no one mentioned it any more.

ᴐᴑᴖᴑᴖᴑᴖᴑᴖᴑᴖᴑᴖᴑᴖᴑᴖᴑᴖᴑᴐ *4*

Now, it had become a matter of urgency. In the times before, talk of my father's going home had always faltered as much from a sense of no immediacy as anything else. Slowly, through the years, the family had succumbed to his seeming reluctance to carry out his spoken plans and had come to adopt his attitude that perhaps next year would be better at that.

But as my brother Paul said, this was the end of the road for that kind of thinking. What had happened to my father in the hills the month before was something of portent. We could not let him go the way of the others, wanting and waiting and waiting until it was too late, and then living out their last days with unfulfillment a hurt in their hearts.

There was no mistaking that he had had a little stroke. And even though he was recovering and would have had to be in good physical shape to stay in the hills, we knew he should see a doctor. Yet, any idea of persuading him to do so seemed hopeless. My mother gave us fair warning of that. She reminded us of how she had pleaded with him for years to go to a doctor about his rupture. Then one night, when my father was at table with his herders in the winter cabin, it had finally burst. And, even then, he had said nothing but had gone out into the night and crawled under a wagon. And he would have stayed there too, if one of the herders had not suspected something and gone out to look for him.

It was a quirk in my father's character that showed us the way, both to the doctor, and, enlarging upon it, to the trip. When we thought about it, we saw for the first time why it was that he kept certain appointments and not others. Quite unconsciously, because he was our father and very much of a man unto himself, we had granted him the right to make his own appointments. We had not taken it upon ourselves to make them for him, because each in our own way, even though we had never thought about it, felt that it would be wrong.

But, in the rare times when it had happened by accident, we remembered that he had met his appointments faithfully, that he had actually seemed frightened to death of missing them. What we had to come to accept as his unpredictable nature was really not that at all. It was a matter of who made the appointment. The reason he did not make his own was because of his unwillingness to cope with a strange modern world of official designations. But once such a designation had been made, once he was bound by a stated time and someone from that impersonal world was depending upon him, he would rather cut off his arm than miss it.

And as we pursued it, we realized that this had always been the stumbling block in his plans for going home. Each time, the prospect of making the arrangements had overwhelmed him, and, with too much pride to ask for help, he had invented the responsibilities that forever postponed his trip.

It was with no little glee that the family leaped to the undertaking. Suddenly, all the timeworn hopes of my father's return to the old country became new and real. Within a few days, his every move for the next three months was charted by appointment. He had an appointment to see the federal court clerk about his citizenship papers, another with the county clerk to apply for his passport, another with the doctor for his shots and a long overdue examination. He had plane reservations all the way to Bordeaux and back, and, taking him at his word, tickets to the Marciano-LaStarza fight in New York City. And, while the excitement raged, my father was in the hills herding his sheep, blissfully unaware of his busy future.

There were still problems, however. Despite the intricate planning by which we would personally put my father on the plane in San Francisco and my brother John—who was in law school in Washington, D.C.—would take him off in New York City, escort him to the fight, and put him back on the plane to France, there was a danger.

My mother insisted that, with my father's ignorance of the ways of airports and schedules, he was certain to miss connections somewhere along the way. What was worse, she was also convinced that, with his habit of talking to strangers, he would be led astray in Paris, and, as she put it, get knocked over the head by some villainous Apache, and as a result never make it to the Pyrenees. Finally, to compound all this, she had a passionate conviction that, once my father had returned to the country of his birth, he would never come back to America. Though the family argued this heatedly, my mother was sure that we would never see him again.

"Listen to me," she prophesied solemnly, "you don't know these Basques like I do. Once he is there where he began, he will forget he ever lived in this country!"

Of course, the logical solution to this dilemma would have been for my mother to accompany my father on the trip. Since she had handled the business affairs of the family ever since we could remember and was well versed in the ways of travel, she should have been the natural one to go. But, from the beginning, she had never wanted to return, and now, in spite of her fears, she was just as adamant against going as she ever had been. This was her country now, and this was her home, she said, and France was only a memory of a life long past.

So, it was decided that I would be my father's traveling companion, first to see that he got there, and, last, to make sure he came back.

It was a time of rest and reunion for the sheepherders. The bands had been brought down from the high mountains to the valley ranch, and after the long trail drive the business of mouthing and separating the ewes was a slow and easy task.

It was a time of conversation and visiting. The soft flow of Basque filled the corrals and the bunkhouse. Although they rose at daylight and worked in the corrals until the long noonday rest, they paused often in the milling dust to lean against a fence and tip back their sweaty hats and visit. They spoke of how their bands had fared in the mountains and where the feed was good and of their dogs and the endless troubles with the burros. They spoke of the outfit and how they treated their men, and of the time the camptender who brought the supplies had committed the unpardonable sin of forgetting the wine. And how they were treated was important because they were Basques and their pride was their flaming shield, and they took insult from no man.

At nightfall, when the evening meal was done, there was a campfire under the trees and the wine *chahakoa* made the circle often, and there was talk of home and their people and the melancholy songs of the Pyrenees. The time of aloneness in the mountains was passed, and it was reunion, and in a few days this too would pass and they would be wending their ways into the high country again, alone.

It was noonday and the valley camp was lulled when we came to see my father. The herders were resting on their cots in the bunkhouse, and the sheepdogs dozed in the cool shade. Not wanting to sleep inside, my father had pitched his bed under a cottonwood tree, and he was lying on it when we came.

It did not take him long to sense something was afoot, but he was not quite sure what. He had surrendered the bed to my mother, who perched on the edge and regarded him with a knowing smile. My father was sitting on the grass with his back against the tree, and we sat in a circle about him. After a while, his conversation began to falter, and his eyes narrowed from time to time as he caught a poorly concealed grin.

My brother Paul, who was a district attorney at a young age, maneuvered him into talk of the trip in his deftest courtroom manner. He began with questions about the letter from the old country, and then remarked casually, "Robert was saying you were thinking about a trip back there."

"Well, they said she wanted to see me pretty bad," my father said hesitantly.

"But now wouldn't be a very good time to go, would it?" said Paul. "The sheep will be heading back into the hills soon, and you'll have to go with them, won't you?"

"Oh, I don't hardly have to go back to the hills," my father protested, abandoning his caution. "I was talking to the foreman, and he said they was going to bunch the ewes and I could get off for a while if I wanted to."

"But the weather will be miserable back there now," argued my brother. "Isn't the spring the best time?"

"No, no," said my father. "It happens to rain too much in the spring back there and the roads and the trails are muddy. The autumn is always the prettiest time."

"Well, why don't you go back then, Pop?"

"I been thinking about it, all right," said my father gravely.

"Do you want to go back?"

"You know I had a notion to go back for a long time, Paul," said my father.

"Maybe you'd better wait until next year," argued Paul. "Maybe next year would be better for you."

"No, no," said my father, shaking his head. "Now would be the best time."

"Well, that's what we thought, Pop," said Paul with a grin. "And since you were so busy, we went ahead and made the arrangements."

It took a few moments before the realization of what Paul had said dawned on my father. And then disbelief and quick fright passed across his features. He forced a little laugh and shrugged away what he had heard.

"But I'm serious, Pop," said Paul. "You have reservations on the plane for September." And then, he quietly related in sequence the schedule of my father's appointments for the next few weeks.

My father struggled nobly with his emotions as he felt the trap drawing tighter. Throwing up his hands, he made one last struggle. "That's nice, Paul," he said. "But what am I going to do? That's rough country where the sheep are going, and some of these young herders can't take care of them the way they should." He nodded his head decisively as he spoke. "I got to herd them for a while anyway." He brightened for an instant. "Maybe next year," he began.

"But, Pop," said Paul, looking at my father with tragic helplessness, "the reservations have been made."

My father slumped as though the world had settled on his shoulders. "*O yoi, Jesu,*" he said hopelessly, and gave up the struggle.

But though he had accepted the fact of the trip, he refused to talk about it any more, turning away all mention of it and talking furiously about nothing in particular. And so we too did not speak of it any more that day, but gave him grace to taste it a little at a time, and in his own privacy. When we left, and he said good-by, the beginning of it was already in his eyes.

"It's a funny thing," my father said. "But here it is forty-seven years later and my life is almost over and I'm going back. When I came, it was to be for just a little while, just enough time to make some money and go back and help Papa and Mamma with the care of the property. I was the baby in the family, you know, and the last one home with Marie-Jeanne. Both your Uncle Pêtes was here in America, and the others was married to other properties and gone. And it was up to me to help the old folks."

He threw up his leathered hands and held them before him with the fingers wide. "But what could I do?" he demanded with a passion as though it were yesterday. "What chance was there if I stayed? There was no money for anything. I wanted stock and the land to move in," he said, "and we didn't even own the property where we lived."

Later, he said, "We went around and made our

good-bys. There was myself and Jean, my friend. Every-one in Tardets was excited, because you know there was only a few who had ever gone away from our town." He was quiet for a long time. Then he said, "I re-member when it came the time to say good-by to Papa and Mama at the old property. Papa was a strong man and he never cried, even when our brother drowned in the river, but he kissed me and he picked up dirt in his fingers and pressed it hard into my hand, and he said, 'Remember, this is your country. Come back to it.' And when I held my mother for the last time, I said to her, 'Mama, Mama, I'll come back in a little while.' But she must of known what was to happen, because all she would say was, '*Adieu, mon petit. Adieu. Adieu.*' "

He was going back, and it was as hard for the others to realize as it was for him. They had lived so long in America that the old country had become a dimming dream in which little things stood out and the rest was blurred, but beautifully, because it was of memory. They had become so used to the uncertain images of letters that they could not comprehend that soon he was to see with his own eyes, that he was to walk in the vil-lages of their youth and talk with their people of yesterday.

Now was the time for rekindled hopes of going home in those who still were able, and a time of sadness for those who could not. Now was the time when women went to their rooms and looked again at nearly forgot-ten pictures of home and wept quiet tears, and lonely men lay on their beds and longed for the voices of their childhood.

In the days that remained, my father visited with his countrymen and took their commissions. There were notes of greeting scrawled laboriously on bits of paper by men who had not written a letter since they came, because they were afraid of such things as post offices and the formal demands of correct address. There were the private letters of women in beautiful old-country script, and there were pictures of sons and daughters born in America, who looked like any other American sons and daughters. And there were newspaper clippings telling of the deaths of a husband or wife and what they had done in America and the fact that they had been natives of France or Spain, and, underlined in pencil, the names of the villages of their birth in the Pyrenees, all of which my father would have to interpret for the people in the old country, because it was in English.

There was a small Basque hotel in a little town in the next valley. My father had stopped to make a visit, and, as was the custom of the sheepmen, had bought a round of drinks for the house. All those who drank were Basque, and most of them old sheepmen, or sheepherders who had come to town for their two weeks out of the year. And each had his own reason why he had never returned.

There was Jean Baptiste, who had owned his sheep and had sold them and had money, who laughed and slapped his legs and roared, "*A la Jinkoa,* Dominique! I think I'll go back myself."

My father said, "Then come back with us. We can make the arrangements like that," and he snapped his fingers.

But Jean Baptiste laughed and shook his head violently. "*Ez, ez, ez!*" he protested. "Too busy, too busy. Next year I'll go. You tell them I'm coming back next year."

There was St. Martin, who was a bartender and who had wanted to go back, but not until he had enough money to buy a property near his town and marry a Basque girl. But he had wanted a good time in this country too, and when he had finally saved enough money to go back, he was too old for a wife, and it had made him bitter. "What do you want to go back for, Dominique?" he said. "Nothing has changed back there. You know what it's like. You're not going to see anything new."

There was Gilian, who had had a girl and a property waiting for him long ago. He was a sheepherder with too much pride, and when he came to town for his two weeks a year, he had tried to act like a property owner already, and spent all his wages buying drinks for the house, and gone back to the mountains broke every time. "Dominique," he said, still carrying the air of a landowner, "you go see that property for me. They tell me it's in bad shape now." He curled his mouth and said, "That's what happens when men don't know how to run a property." About the girl who lived on the property with her husband of many years he said nothing, because he had too much pride for that too.

There was Tristant, who had worked for the same man for twenty years after he came to this country, and who had never taken his two weeks but stayed always with the sheep, because he did not want to risk spending his money. And because he did not know the ways of banks, he had told the sheepman for whom he worked to keep track of his wages and pay him when he was ready to go back to the old country. At the end of twenty years, he would have had good money, but the sheepman went broke and could pay him only a hundred dollars. After that, Tristant had given up and never saved another cent, but went to town every year for his two weeks and drank in sullen and brooding silence until his money was gone.

There was Joanes *Ergela,* or Crazy John, who had lost his mind from loneliness in the mountains and had not seen it coming soon enough to shoot himself, as the others like him had done. He stood at my father's side like a child and plucked at his sleeve, and whimpered over and over again, "You going back, Dominique? You going back, Dominique? You going back home?"

Later, at a ranch near town, there was old Joanes, who had sent word to my father that he was leaving for the mountains with the sheep that day and wanted to see him. Joanes had saved his money twice. The first time, he had put it in the bank, and then the crash came and the banks closed. The second time, he had saved it in a suitcase. But when he finally quit his job and went to San Francisco to make the arrangements for the trip, a Spaniard from Los Angeles had gotten him drunk and stolen his suitcase. After that, Joanes had given up too.

We stood in the old barn with the earth floor where Joanes had slept while the sheep were in the valley. His bed was on the burro, and the sheep were already bunched and ready to move. "I don't believe you are going, Dominique," he said, "but I cannot take a chance. Go see my sister and tell her not to wait for me any more." He held up an old, gnarled hand. "I cannot bring myself to write it to her."

Then he was silent almost without breathing, because he would say this once and never again to any man. "And, Dominique," he said, "tell her something," and he faltered before he could finish it, "but don't tell her what I have come to at the end of my life."

My father put his hand on the old herder's shoulder and said gently, "*Gaichoa,* Joanes."

And then he was gone, without saying good-by, his *makila* in his hand and his dog at his heels, and we stood by the old barn while the sheep began to move toward the silent mountains, and the dust of their moving had swallowed him up.

He could understand buying the hat, because all the stiffness had gone out of the old Stetson and the sweat had pushed its way into the wide brim. But he absolutely could not see the need for a new suit.

"Why, it's durned near brand-new," he said, referring to the wedding suit that hung in the closet at home. "I looked at it the other day, and there ain't even a worn place on it. That's a good suit, you know. I paid an awful lot of money for it back when we got married, and there wasn't a better or a stronger suit in Reno."

He did not have to remind us how strong it was. There was no denying the quality of the material that went into it. That was the trouble. It was like a suit of armor, and another thirty years would have as little effect on it as the first thirty years had.

"But, Pop," we argued, "don't you think it might be

a little bit old-fashioned? Times have changed quite a bit since then, you know."

"*Bho!*" he said, waving the objection aside with one hand. "A suit's a suit, and," he added, "it's durned near brand-new."

"We know that, Pop, and we're not saying it isn't a beautiful suit. But you take that coat Paul's got on, for example. Do you notice how the cut of it goes, how the lapels are wider, and how the shoulders—"

My father used both hands this time. "So long as it's clean," he said, "no one notices those things."

There was a pause as we parried for another opening, and then, like an inspiration, "Yes, but, Pop, you should have another suit for a change, like when we get to New York and want to go to the fights, and this one will be all wrinkled from the plane trip."

It was a good argument, because it made an impression. He thought for a moment, and, while he was thinking, I said, "And what if you spill something on it in the plane? Those things happen all the time in the air."

"Well," he said, weakening rapidly, "it seems to me a little hot water and—"

"Sure, Pop, but you shouldn't take a chance of hurting that material. You don't want to ruin a suit like that."

"Well—" he began.

"Well, let's at least go in and see what they have. If you don't like anything you try on, we'll let it go at that," we concluded quickly, knowing that if the chances were right and the salesman was a good one, my father would not have the heart to turn him down.

41

We were still riding the crest of good luck. The salesman was not only a good one, but he was an old-timer too, and that put my father at ease. It was not very long before they found they had many friends in common from the old days in Reno. And, all the while, the salesman was helping my father in and out of suit coats.

With the first few suits, my father simply wrinkled his brow in mild disapproval, and the salesman quickly removed them and helped him on with another. Then, finally, there was one for which his brow remained placid and even interested. It was dark and it hung well on his wide shoulders and lean frame.

"Well, I don't know," he said reluctantly. "It's a pretty-looking suit and all that, but it seems to me like it might be a waste of money." Then he proceeded to tell the salesman about the wedding suit he had bought in Reno for an awful lot of money back then.

For a few moments, the day was almost lost, because the salesman's eyes brightened and he said, "Hey, I remember hearing about that suit. I was just a young man in the clothing business then, and I remember everyone talking about it." And he went on, describing the material that had gone into it, and the unheard-of price, and how all the tailors in town had dropped around to admire it.

"You're right," my father said, starting to get out of the new coat. "It's a good suit, and I don't need another."

For an instant, the salesman looked befuddled, and then recovered himself almost miraculously from the error of his nostalgic remembering. "Oh, no!" he said, shaking his head gravely. "Never trust those old suits.

You think they're going to last forever, and then one day," and he exploded his hands, "poof!"

"Is that right?" my father said seriously.

"I'm telling you," the salesman said with his hand on his heart, and he had made a sale.

Walking into Parker's was like walking into old Reno. This was the store where the stockmen went, and had gone from the beginning, when Reno was a stockman's town. There was the smell of new denim and leather, with the levis piled on the counters as high as a man could see, leather boots in no special order in the window, and Stetsons stacked in the corners one upon the other, clear to the ceiling.

"*Nola zida,* Dominique," said Abe, who had appeared as if by magic from behind one of the piles of levis.

"You talk like an *Eskualduna,*" said my father.

"I should," said Abe, who had been around the Basque sheepmen so long he had conquered some of their expressions. "It's my second tongue."

"You must be trying to get to heaven, then," said my father.

"Meaning what?" said Abe warily.

"Well, you know what they say about the devil," said my father. "He spent a thousand years trying to learn the language so he could tempt them, and then he gave it up, and that's why no Basques ever go to hell."

"I've got my doubts about that," said Abe, and they grinned as men who have understood each other for a long time.

"Same color?" asked Abe, and, without waiting for

my father's answer, he neatly jerked a hatbox from the middle of the pile. The towering column dropped down, wobbled a little on the top, and then was still. "Where've you been?" said Abe. "I was expecting you before this." He took the Stetson out of the box, dented the crown in the way my father liked, and handed it to him.

"I been herding sheep," said my father.

"You Basques can't stay away from them, can you?" said Abe. "You eat dirt and dust and walk your legs off for fifty years, and then you get to the time when you can take it easy, and what do you do but go back for more."

"Well, it's the only thing we know how to do," said my father.

"Don't tell me that," said Abe. "It's the only thing you want to do."

"Well, it's like the story about the Mexican sheepherder," my father said. "He would fight with his burro from the morning until the night every day, and he was always complaining to his camptender about it. So the camptender got tired of listening and happened to ask him one day why he didn't get himself a new burro, and the Mexican sheepherder said, 'But why should I? I like him.'"

"The last time I heard that one was from a Mexican," said Abe, "and it was about a Basque sheepherder."

That tickled my father and he threw back his head and laughed delightedly. They bantered for a while, and then my father said, "Jesus crackers, but this hat will see something, all right. I'm going back to the old country, you know."

"Oh," said Abe, with the tone of one who had been through this before.

"I mean it," said my father, and he produced the plane tickets from the pocket of his leather jacket.

"I'll be darned, Dominique!" said Abe, startled. "I never thought I would see the day when one of you *Eskualdunac* meant it."

"Well, I got nothing to do now," said my father, and there was a shadow of wistfulness in his voice. "I don't have my sheep any more."

"I know," sighed Abe. "Nobody's got any sheep any more. The sheep are going, and I don't like to see it," he said, frowning. "I can remember the day, and that was when you were big too, when we did business with twenty-five outfits, and right around Reno alone. And now," and he opened his hands as if throwing something into the wind, "they're gone."

"It's a sad thing to say," my father said. "But the market is going, and the ranges are getting chopped up, and the young men don't want to work in the hills, and you can't hardly blame them, I guess. In a lot of ways, it wasn't a pretty life back then."

"It's more than that," said Abe with conviction. "They don't raise the same kind of people. Those were big men back in those days. They couldn't cover country in a car or an airplane maybe, but right from where they were sitting on a horse, they could think bigger and do bigger than any people I've ever seen."

As they talked and remembered, the Reno that was seemed to live again. It was like a breath out of the past that one could see and feel and hear and even smell, when Commercial Row and Lake Street were dirt, and

45

the cattle names were Mapes and Moffat and Murdock, and sheep meant men like Sario and Poco and Flannagan, and all these names and all these places were said with an old familiarity that belongs only to those who had said them long ago.

This was a time when gaslights still flickered on the street corners, and the clump of boots could be heard in the stores and in saloons with old high bars of dark mahogany, and outside in the night the plodding echo of a solitary horse. This was a time when bankers and businessmen in high white collars talked big money with dusty men who smelled of leather and sagebrush, and money in Reno still had a soul in it, because these men had fought for it with sweat and blood and honest toil. This was the old Reno that they talked of and remembered and knew, before its heart had begun to die.

ananananananananananan **6**

The big, four-engined TWA plane taxied to the end of the runway and turned with graceful ease. There were a few moments when the plane was still and the engines idled, and I stole a glance at my father. He was sitting rigidly in his seat, but there was an expression on his face as though to say, "Well, that wasn't so bad."

In anticipation of what was to come, I spoke to him, but he shook his head shortly in a signal that he did not want to talk. When I tried to make him peer through the window for a last glimpse of the family waving good-by, he acted as if he had not heard me.

The pilot began to rev his engines and the plane trembled and shook with tremendous surges of power. Then, suddenly, the steel tube in which we were sealed was hurtling down the runway, and the air terminal and the hangars and the hills of San Francisco were a blur in the windows. My father was like a man facing execution. His face was set as stonily as an Indian's, and his hands were clamped on the armrest so tightly that the knuckles showed white.

There was a lift as the plane became airborne and the ground swept away from under us. Beneath his deep tan, my father went pale. His legs twitched and his fingers worked helplessly on the armrests, as though his body were powerless to understand that it was a captive, that this was not a thing like a bucking horse that it could fight with hands and legs.

In a little while, the plane reached its cruising altitude, and the engine roar settled down to a lulling drone. The hostesses began to move about with cheerful smiles, and one even tried to get my father to look out the window. He refused in no uncertain fashion. Throughout the plane, passengers picked up magazines and started to relax as casually as if they were in their own homes. The seat in front of us lowered so suddenly that my father started. He leaned forward in amazement and saw that its occupant, a lady of more than middle age, was getting ready to take a nap.

"I'll be durned," he said. But after that, he too stretched out his legs and even managed a smile of sorts.

"How do you like it, Pop?" I asked.

He lifted his shoulders. "I like it," he said, "at least so far. But I sure got worried about my stomach there for a while." He leaned close and put his hand over his mouth to conceal his lips. "I don't know what I would of done if it happened to me."

"People get airsick all the time," I said.

He groaned. "Oh no," he said. "I would of rather died than in front of all these people."

It wasn't until we had passed the hump of the Sierra

and were over Nevada that he would venture even an angled glance through the window. But when he did, something caught his eye immediately and his brow furrowed. "I know that peak," he said, pointing to a mountain whose top had a strange indentation on one side, as if something had taken a bite out of it. "I made my camp in that funny hollow one night. There's a pretty little spring of water in it, you know."

"Well, we're over Nevada," I said.

He was incredulous. "Good God, I can't hardly believe it," he said. "Once when I got mixed up, it took me days to cross that desert on hossback, and the pack mare couldn't make it and I had to shoot the poor thing. By the time I got to that peak and found the water, my tongue was so big it filled my mouth."

Then, in rapid succession, he saw other ranges and deserts, each of which seemed to call up a time out of the past. There was a narrow canyon where the sheep had been trapped by an early snow so deep that it covered the entire band. He had made his way out alone and on foot through the choking drifts until he reached the main camp, and then they had taken all their horses and tied them neck to neck, and gone back and whipped them down into the gorge and up again and back again, until there was a hard-packed trail through the snow that the sheep could travel to escape. But, even then, they had had to take a dead ewe that had been smothered and tie her in a standing position to a long tree limb and drag her behind a horse, so that the other sheep would follow.

Later, there was a range of twisted desert mountains, where he had herded sheep soon after he had come to this country. There had been an outlaw cabin there for a band of cattle rustlers and bandits, and, because he was still a boy and could speak just a few words of English and was the only other human being in that remote range, they had come to know each other. He could remember watching them shoot at cans and knots in the corral fences with their long pistols, and their limping leader, George Davis, was the best of them all. Many years later, my father was to recognize the familiar limp of George Davis at the state prison farm near Carson City, and, later again, learn that he had died an old man, in prison.

When the land of Nevada was behind us, he lapsed into a long silence. After a while, he said, "It's a funny thing. Now that I'm going home, I try to think about the old country and days before I came here, but it seems that what's in my mind is the early time in Nevada."

"Maybe it's because the suffering began here."

"Maybe," he said, "but I don't hardly think so. I don't remember much suffering, except for when I first came, and that was from something else. You would have to see the beauty of the Basque country before you knew what I meant, but I remember going out into that cruel desert when I first came, and nights when I cried to sleep in my tent. But afterward it wasn't suffering, because it was the way things was, and a man couldn't do anything about it, and maybe that's why he didn't spend the time thinking about it, either."

The great hump of the Rockies rose before us, and we could look down and see green forests that turned to slate blue on the shadow side of the mountains, and streams that were like silver veins in the sunlight, and entire slopes on which wild flowers grew in splashes of color.

"This was the dividing line, it seemed like then," my father said. "When we was coming on the train, most everything seemed to change right here. The country got bigger and the mountains was higher, and you could look for miles without seeing a fence. Even the people had a different look to them. They had color in their faces, and they didn't dress very fancy. You saw work clothes, and the others looked like they was wearing their Sunday suits. I remember we liked these mountains here and the people, and we were sorry it wasn't Nevada and we could get off."

"Were they friendlier here?" I asked.

He nodded. "Yes, they was. They took us for granted more. In the East, they was a little funny. I remember on the train, they wouldn't talk but they would just sit and look at us for an hour without saying a word. There was one stout man in a suit, I remember, who made me uncomfortable as hell. Every time I turned around, he was staring at us, just sitting and staring without offering to talk. I was sure glad when he got off the train."

"They didn't make fun of you, did they?" I said.

"No," he said. "Most of them was all right." A grin came slowly to his face. "But there was two young fellows who did." The grin broadened and he shook his head, remembering. "They got on the train in this one town, and they sat right across the aisle from us. It happened to be my turn to sit next to the window, and Jean, my friend who died, was sitting on the seat nearest them.

"One of these fellows did most of the talking. He was

dressed in a nice suit, but he was sort of sickly looking. Maybe he'd been drinking, I don't know. He seen us right away, and I remember him laughing not very quiet. At first, his friend didn't look like he wanted to get into it, but he did after a while too. I don't know what the hell was so funny, but I guess it was our clothes and the way we looked. And everytime we talked in Basque, this sickly-looking one would laugh like hell, so we was afraid to open our mouths any more."

"Why didn't you punch him?"

"No," my father said. "When you come to a new country, you can't do things like that, and you don't want to anyway. That would be the last thing you would think of doing." He was serious for a moment, and then the grin returned. "But I'll tell you what Jean, my late friend, did do."

The mountains had ended and we were flying high over the plains, and the air seemed to be more turbulent than before. My father shifted uncomfortably a few times, and then shrugged his shoulders as if resigning himself to it, and resumed his story.

"After a while, when we wouldn't talk," he said, "and this fellow didn't have anything new to laugh at, he tried something else. He would lean across the aisle and talk real serious to us in English, just like he was discussing something important with us. Of course, we didn't answer because we couldn't understand him. But he would make out like we had answered, and would nod his head like we had said something important and he was thinking about it, and then he would start talking again, on and on.

"His friend must of thought that was funny, because

52

he started laughing too, and pretty soon we could hear some of the other people sort of snickering. The conductor, though, who was a nice fellow and could talk a little Canadian French, looked mad. He said something once to them, but they kept on anyway.

"You must remember," he went on, "that Jean, my friend, was a good boy. He was always easygoing and happy and never in trouble. But he happened to be dark and he had a long face and black eyes, and sometimes for fun he could twist his face up and drop one of his eyelids and make his mouth to disappear, and it looked so durned mean it would scare you to see him.

"Anyway, he made his face that way now, and he reached under the seat real slow and pulled out his clothes sack. The American fellow stopped talking for a minute, and then he stopped altogether so he could watch what Jean was doing.

"When he had the sack in front of him, Jean untied the string as slow as you please and reached inside and took out this Spanish knife that was a wicked thing to see. He didn't hurry one bit. He put the knife on his lap and reached in and got his sharpening stone and put that on his lap too."

The stewardess stopped by to ask my father how he was enjoying his trip, and when he said that he was, she moved to the next seat. My father went on.

"I asked Jean what the hell he was doing, and he whispered it to me. I didn't laugh, but kept my face straight, and I looked real quick across the aisle, and they was watching Jean without saying a word, and they didn't look very happy now.

"Jean sharpened his knife on the stone, testing it on

53

his thumb every once in a while and then sharpening it some more. When he was done, he put the sharpening stone back in the sack and pulled out this little bundle that was in there. Then he put the knife and the bundle on his lap and started to roll up his sleeves, just like he didn't want to get any blood on them.

"When he was done, he picked up the knife in one hand and the bundle in the other. Then he got up real quick and stepped across the aisle." My father paused and laughed aloud. "I never saw anything like it. One of them started shouting and the other went to climb over the seats to get away. The conductor came running up, and he looked a little afraid of that knife too, but he asked Jean in his patois what he was doing. And Jean showed him the bundle in his other hand, and said in French, 'I was offering them some bread and cheese.'

"The conductor must of thought that was funny as hell, because he bent right over laughing. And then he said something to the two young American fellows, and I guess he asked them if they wanted some bread and cheese, because right then everybody in the train started laughing like hell too.

"Well," my father said, "they didn't take any, of course, and they didn't bother us any more, but I never saw two men look so durned mad in all my life."

He leaned his head back and grinned at the ceiling of the plane. "Maybe it wasn't a nice thing to do, to scare them like that. But I couldn't hardly ever get mad at Jean, because he didn't have a mean bone in his body. Later, when he got killed in our trouble on the range, I used to remember what happened on the train, and I couldn't get mad at all."

Despite our finest hopes, my father arrived in New York City in his wedding suit. And, at that, it was a good compromise. Because for one harrowing instant while he was packing in Carson City, he thought he would "durn well save the suit," and make the trip in his boots, levis, and jumper. But my mother put her foot down on that, and so he reluctantly agreed to pack all these, with spares. When he boarded the plane, his baggage was forty pounds overweight.

Tucked away in his suitcase, and still in the tissue paper and long box in which it had come, was the beautiful new suit he had bought in Reno. It seemed as though it was there to stay, because when he had packed he had pronounced his fatal epitaph on it: "I think I'll save this for a while." This meant, of course, that, if he had his way, the new suit would remain in the box all the way to France, all the time we were there, and for years afterward.

55

So it was that my father came to New York looking for all the world like an old-time country squire, with a broad-brimmed hat, high shoes and narrow trousers, and a coat with big pockets that flared at the skirt. He must have looked as threatening as a squire, because, after we had landed in New York, one colored porter refused to carry our bags. And he went away, glancing back every once in a while with a sober expression.

Perhaps what gave the porter misgivings were the bulges in my father's suit. They came from little bundles. There was a bundle of snapshots he had promised to deliver to the families of his friends, another of letters and notes, some sagebrush leaves from the desert, a shiny silver dollar for the wife of a young Spanish herder, a chunk of gold ore he had found in the mountains, and rattlesnake rattles of various sizes and number, each with a history.

The biggest bundle of all was made up of his wallet and the passport folder the travel agency had given him. With the exception of this bundle, all the rest were wrapped carefully in paper and tied with bits of string, just as they would have been in the mountains. As far back as we could remember, my father was forever picking up scraps of paper and string for just this purpose. Probably because string and paper were always precious in the mountains, it bothered him no end to see them wasted.

The bundle that was the wallet and passport folder was wrapped with extra care. It was bound with a heavy, black inner-tube band used to deliver the San Francisco *Chronicle* at home, and then, for maximum security, with a thick string cord.

None of the myriad other little bundles would he pack in his suitcase, because he did not trust "them." He was dead certain "they" would manage to lose or misplace his baggage somewhere along the way, and these bundles were more valuable to him than anything else.

In the hotel room in New York City, we sat and marveled at the bundles and how he had managed to carry all of them in one suit. My father was taking a bath, because even though he hated to "waste the water," he felt like cleaning up before going out to dinner. My brother John, who was a law student in Washington, D.C., had come to meet us and see our plane off to France. That night, he was going to guide us to a nice place for dinner, and afterward we would all see the Marciano-LaStarza fight at the Polo Grounds.

The bundles were stacked neatly on the bed, and the wedding suit was draped on a hanger, "to give it a rest." John hefted some of the bundles in his hands, and then got up and dropped a few of them in the pockets of the wedding suit. They vanished in the dark depths, and he dropped a few more in.

"I guess it's possible," he said. "The darned thing must be all pocket." He put the bundles back on the bed and stood back to survey the suit. Then he took the coat off the hanger and tried it on. He was tall, with the same long and lean frame as my father, and it was a fairly good fit. He stood in front of the mirror and looked at himself. "You can't tell," he said. "In a few more years, this might be back in style."

"One thing," I said. "You can be sure it'll still be as good as new."

John felt the cloth of the coat in his fingers. "I can't understand why it doesn't wear out," he mused. "I wonder if they used steel thread in those days."

"Let's get back to the problem," I said. "How are we going to get him into the new suit." I listened for the sound of splashing from the bathroom. "We've got only about ten minutes, you know."

John put the coat to the wedding suit back on its hanger, and then took the coat to the new suit out of its box and tried that on. "This is a nice suit," said John. "Why in the devil doesn't he like it?"

"Oh, he likes it," I said. "He's crazy about the thing. It's just that he wants to save it."

There was no need for further explanation. John understood perfectly. "Did I ever tell you?" he said. "The last time I was home, I was up in the attic room looking for some stuff, and what do you think I found?"

"I've got a good idea," I said.

"That's right," said John. "I found a whole drawer full of shirts and gloves and sweaters that we'd given him for Christmas and birthdays for ten years past, and every one of them was brand-new."

"Well, he's saving them," I said by way of explanation.

"Yeah," said John.

We sat on the bed and looked at the wedding suit. It loomed as indestructible as chain mail. John lit a cigarette and held the burning match in front of him and regarded it. "Fire," he murmured aloud.

"Well," I said. "He packed everything except a carbine, so you're pretty safe. If you think you're in good enough shape for fighting, go ahead."

John blew out the match. "No, that's too drastic." He sighed and reached for the phone. "There's always a gentleman's way out." He called the desk and asked for the valet to come up to the room immediately.

He came, even as we were listening apprehensively to the sounds from the bathroom, where my father was drying himself. John handed the suit to the valet. "We'd like to have this cleaned," he said.

The valet turned the suit around on its hanger. "That's good material," he said.

"Yes, we know," said John, and closed the door behind him.

It was just in time, because no sooner had he left than the bathroom door opened and my father came out in his long underwear. "I thought I heard a stranger's voice in here," he said.

"It was the valet," said John.

My father put his shaving kit on the dresser and turned around to reach for the wedding suit. A look of perplexity crossed his brow, and then he strode over to the closet. I lighted a cigarette nervously.

"Where did I put it?" my father said.

"What?" said John.

"My suit," my father said. "The durned thing's gone!"

John maintained his composure. "Oh, you mean your old one, Pop?" he said casually. "We gave it to the valet. Thought you'd like to have it nice and clean for the trip to France."

My father came out of the closet. I was engrossed in a newspaper and John was lying on the bed, smoking and looking at the ceiling. There was a silence, and I will

59

never know what my father was thinking at that moment.

"That's just fine," he said, finally. "And now, what am I going to wear tonight?"

John propped himself up on an elbow. "Don't you have another suit?" he asked puzzledly. "I thought you bought another suit."

My father threw his hands up in the air. "But it's brand-new."

"I don't understand what you mean, Pop," said John, mildly.

"Well, I wanted to—" my father began, and stopped short. "Oh hell, nothing." He walked over to his bag and opened the box and gently eased out the new suit coat.

"Is that it?" said John excitedly. "That's a beauty, Pop. Try it on and let me see how it looks."

"Do you think so?" my father said, and slipped the coat on over his long underwear. John swung his legs over the side of the bed and surveyed him critically. "It was made for you, Pop," he said with conviction.

"It is a pretty suit, all right," my father agreed.

"A lot nicer than the old one," ventured John.

"Well, I don't know about that," my father began.

"Anyway, it sure looks good on you," interrupted John quickly.

"I guess maybe it does," said my father, returning to the mirror and running his hands over the lapels. "But it's a durned shame to wear it."

"Well," John slipped, "there's nothing else you can do now."

My father regarded him from under his deep brows. "I guess not," he said, and looked to where I was still hiding behind the newspaper. "You," he said. "What's so durned interesting in that paper?"

"Oh, nothing," I said.

"That's what I figured," said my father.

Nothing he could have worn would have made any difference. He was as out of place in this New York café as the tuxedoed waiter would have been in a dusty horse corral. In this dimly lighted gathering of well-groomed people with soft faces and hands, he was an oddity with a leathered and creased face and hands that looked more like darkened wood than flesh.

As we entered the café and followed the headwaiter to the table, people turned and watched. Some regarded him with curious expressions, and a few with a resentment for which they could probably not find words. There was one, a pretty and tailored lady just beginning to gray, whose eyes softened, as if she could remember an old country father with a graven face, who had been a workingman too.

And yet, in spite of this scrutiny, my father was not ill at ease. Instead, he was as interested in the people about him as they were in him. He sat there as quietly and detachedly as if he were in a darkened movie house, observing everything and everyone in the café. His expression was as rapt as a child's, and he was having just as much fun.

The waiters seemed to intrigue him the most. His eyes followed them relentlessly as they moved about, taking in their stiff shirt fronts and black ties and short jackets, and, mostly, the stiff correctness of their manner.

It was inevitable that my father's first altercation

would be with a waiter. The warning came when we ordered a drink before dinner, and my father asked for a little glass of claret. He held up his thumb and forefinger to designate that he wanted "a short one." The waiter looked twice, and then smiled in understanding.

We made it through the soup and the salad without incident. It began when the waiter came to take away our salad plates and put on others for the main course. He collected John's and mine, and then reached for my father's. But he could not lift it, because my father was holding it to the table with both hands.

"I'm sorry," said the waiter. "I thought you were finished."

"I am finished," said my father.

"Oh," said the waiter, and again reached for the salad plate. My father held on.

"May I take your plate, sir?" said the waiter.

"No," said my father mildly.

The waiter stood in confused silence for a moment. "But I have to put another plate there, sir."

My father shook his head. "It's all right," he said. "Don't go to any bother."

The waiter blinked, and then smiled weakly. "Oh, it's no bother at all," he said, and again reached for the plate.

This time, my father put his hands over the plate to protect it. The waiter stopped short and straightened up. He looked at us in something akin to frenzy, and John gestured with his head. The waiter retreated to the back of the room and stood there watching us from long distance. He was pale and he still had a plate in his hands.

"Pop," said John. "Why don't you give him your plate?"

My father shrugged. "It's clean enough," he said.

This time John blinked. "I don't understand what you mean."

"They shouldn't waste a plate," said my father. "This one's fine."

John regarded my father for a long moment. "It's really no bother," he said. "They've got a washer back there that does all the work."

"Well, they might run short," my father said.

"I'm telling you, Pop," said John. "There's no danger." He took a deep drag of his cigarette and leaned forward again. "Pop," he said. "You're going to get that waiter in trouble."

"What?" said my father concernedly.

"It's this way," said John. "They're supposed to put a new plate on for each course. That's the way the management wants it. If the waiter doesn't do it and one of the managers sees him, he gets fired on the spot."

"I never heard of such a thing," my father said.

"It's true," said John. "That waiter's probably worried plenty by now."

"Well, hell," said my father. "Tell him to take it then."

John signaled for the waiter and he came forward. When John nodded his head that it was all right, he reached out gingerly and took the salad plate. "I'm sorry, poor fellow," said my father. "I didn't know you was that close to losing your job."

"Oh, that's all right," said the waiter, comprehending nothing at this stage.

After that, he seemed to expect anything. When dinner was done, my father helped him clear the crumbs from the table by gathering his own into his cupped hand. The waiter merely held out his hand to receive them. When my father was through dropping them in, the waiter said, "Thank you."

And later, when he brought us the check, he stood by with inscrutable countenance as my father pulled his passport and wallet bundle out of his pocket, set it on the table, unwound the black inner-tube band, untied the string, and gave him the money. He also gave him a big tip, and said, "It was a fine dinner. I really enjoyed it. How about you boys?"

And the waiter said in a voice without strength, "Well, I'm very happy."

When we left, John and I turned to look. The waiter was still at the table. His head was bowed and he was resting with both hands braced on the back of a chair.

He may not have been able to understand the manners of a New York café, but he knew a prize fight. This he could understand, because it was old and pure and without guise. On this, he could pronounce judgments like: "He reminds me of Dempsey, this Marciano does. He isn't so clever or quick as Dempsey, but he's got that same killer blood in him. LaStarza is courageous, but he's not the best man. He's whipped already."

As each man who loves a prize fight comes for his own reason, so had he his. It was the reason why they came out of the hills of early Nevada—prospectors and buckaroos and sheepherders on foot and horseback—all come to watch a fight. Because this was something they knew. Like the men in the ring, they too had stood alone and fought alone, with their only weapons the hands that God gave them, and the fight was everything they had ever done and seen and felt. In that square was spoken the only language they understood, undisguised by subtleties and exposed for all the world to see. They saw and recognized the blind and stupid courage of an animal, they saw the beautiful courage of men who were afraid and yet fought, and they saw caution and fatal hesitation and cowardice.

And when it was over, they went away satisfied with the decisive knowledge of victory or defeat. A man had won and a man had been beaten, and the thing was settled, and it was not like the helpless inconclusion of argument.

It was something that all the old country men who had come to a new land could understand. Because they too had had to stand alone and without home to turn to for help, because they had forsaken home, and this was their new country, and they were fighting for acceptance.

It was the reason why we brothers had had to have our baptism of blood in the prize ring. It was the reason why each of us in his own turn, without urging from my father and to the hurt of my mother, had had to find his way alone into that square of light from which there is no escape, to know the terror of being alone and fighting alone, to taste the wild triumph of winning alone, and the bitter and lonely pain of defeat.

It was the reason why the sons of old country people

everywhere must fight a little harder and do something better with their lives. Because we were born of old country people in a new land, and, right or wrong, we had not felt equal to those around us, and had had to do a little more than they in everything we did.

And in that ring were two like us, born of old country people, who had won their battle already, to show the way and that it could be done, to the thousands of sons of old country people who were there watching them.

All of us together were of a generation born of old country people who spoke English with an accent and prayed in another language, who drank red wine and cooked their food in the old country way, and peeled apples and pears after dinner.

We were among the last whose names would tell our blood and the kind of faces we had, to know another language in our homes, to suffer youthful shame because of that language and refuse to speak it, and a later shame because of what we had done, and hurt because we had caused a hurt so deep it could never find words.

And the irony of it was that our mothers and fathers were truer Americans than we, because they had forsaken home and family, and gone into the unknown of a new land with only courage and the hands that God gave them, and had given us in our turn the right to be born American.

And in a little while, even our sons would forget, and the old country people would be only a dimming memory, and names would mean nothing, and the melting would be done.

66

~~~~~~~~~~~~~~~~~~~~~~~~~~~~~~~ *8*

The cabdriver made the first comment on our way to the overseas airport. We had said good-by to John at the hotel, so that he could make an early train back to Washington, and now my father and I were Paris-bound.

The cabdriver was on a tirade about the Puerto Ricans. From the glibness of his talk, it was obvious that this was one of his pet peeves, and that he had covered this ground many times before.

"The damn town's full of 'em," he said. "You'll see when you get to that airport. The place is crawling with 'em." He shook his head and sighed with gubernatorial authority. "I don't know what we're going to do about 'em."

"Well, why are they so much trouble?" I asked, out of curiosity.

He was patient, and showed it. "They're just no damn good. You get next to 'em and you'll find out," he warned. "Pick your pocket in a minute," and he snapped his fingers. A little later, he said, "I'd hate to get caught in a dark alley with some of 'em. Cut your throat just like that!" and he made a kkk sound to illustrate his point.

My father and I both grinned. It was exactly what I had whispered to him about the cabdriver when we first got in.

But he was right about one thing. After we had finished our business at the Air France ticket window and settled down for a wait, we saw that there were indeed a good many Puerto Ricans around. They were coming and going in such a steady flow that I could not understand how so many planes could be landing and taking off. But after a while, we realized that most of them were families coming to greet someone or see them off.

What the cabdriver had said must have made an impression on me, because I noticed that the other people in the terminal seemed to give them a wide berth. And they were indeed dressed differently, with dazzling arrangements of pegged pants and long coats and bright ties. And many of them had knife scars on their faces.

My father had been watching them with no little curiosity. "They don't look so bad," he said.

"Well, I don't know, Pop," I said. "I'd still leave them alone."

I guess I should have remembered a time in Nevada when the Mexican shearing crews came to clip the wool for our sheep, as they did every year for all the outfits. Most times, they were made up of older men who had been on the crews for a long time. But that year there were two young ones with them, who we learned were about twenty years old. After the first few days of working together in the corrals, we came to know them. They were friendly, and at night they would often bring their guitars to the cabin and teach us songs in Spanish. After we came to like them, it came as a shock one night to learn that they both carried knives, that at home in southern California they wore pegged pants and got into knife fights, that they were of the "Pachucos" we had been hearing so much about.

But that had happened in the hills, and things and people are different in the city, or so I thought. I should have known what was to happen, because my father was that way.

No matter where he went, he would strike up a conversation with anybody who happened to be near him. When we first sat down, there was a prosperous-looking man of about my father's age sitting next to us. He had a bulky briefcase and he was reading a newspaper.

When my father first spoke to him, he was genuinely surprised and even a little irritated. But after a few minutes, they were in a lively conversation. My father learned that he was going to England on business, that he did it all the time, and that he knew both Senator Pat McCarran, whom my father knew from the days when the family was in sheep and about whose fieriness in the hills he could tell a few anecdotes, and Senator George Malone, whom my father and my uncle had met on horseback in the deserts many times. And, among other things, my father learned how the export business was doing these days.

A little later, after the businessman had bid him a warm good-by and boarded his plane, my father got into a conversation, first in English and then Italian, with a barber, and he learned all about the barber business both in New York and in Italy, where the man had his start.

All I could do was wonder when the time would come when someone would insult my father for daring to speak to a stranger. The wait for our own plane dragged into hours because of some kind of engine trouble. I stood up from time to time and wandered about the terminal, and once I came back to where my father was sitting to ask him if he wanted another cup of coffee. He didn't, and so I took my leave with the warning, "You know, I don't think I'd fool around with those Puerto Ricans. There's no use taking chances."

My father said nothing, but I had a suspicion then my words were wasted. And I was right. No sooner was I settled in the coffeeshop than I saw through the glass partition that my father was in a conversation with not one, but four of them. If he had chosen them by hand, he could not have picked four more dangerous-looking companions. It must just have started, because from their expressions the Puerto Ricans were still regarding my father with distance. But as I watched, they warmed up to it, and soon they all seemed to be talking and waving their hands at the same time. I knew it had to be in Spanish, because my father could speak that tongue too.

By the time I finished my coffee, they were getting along famously. But when I joined my father, the Puerto Ricans grew a little wary, and things never

70

really got back to where they were, even though all I did was listen.

One of the Puerto Ricans was saying something to my father in Spanish. I groped for the meaning, but could not understand. One of the others, seeing my puzzlement, translated it into English with a thick accent.

"He was saying there is no chance for a Puerto Rican in America."

"But why?" my father asked.

"Because there is nothing we can do here. There is no work, and what there is is no good for a man."

"Then why do you come?" my father asked.

The Puerto Rican lifted his hands. "There is no chance in Puerto Rico either. When we were young, they always said this was a rich land. Maybe it is, but someone else must have it, because we don't. We are tired of waiting to get rich."

"But your people stay here," my father said.

Another of the Puerto Ricans answered him. "Why not? There is nothing else to do. They have no place to go."

"Why don't they go with you?" my father said.

The Puerto Rican shook his head and spoke for a long time, but my translator was more brief. "Brazil is a long way from here and from Puerto Rico too. Some are going, but not many. They do not want to say good-by to their families and their friends, and they do not know what they will find there. They are afraid. And so they live here, millions of them, to be treated worse than a Negro many times. Because the Americans think we are all lazy, that we are criminals, and that we want to live like pigs. But we are human men too, and, even if we have our lazy ones and our criminals, the Americans have them too."

"I don't think they would treat you that way if there were not so many of you, and with nothing to do," my father said.

The first Puerto Rican nodded his head. "That is part of it, all right. But still, it is a hurt not to be thought of as a people with self-respect."

"How do you know it will be different in Brazil?" my father said.

The first Puerto Rican spoke passionately. "This much we know. Brazil is a new country, and the land is rich, rich enough to give a man a good living if he works for it. A Puerto Rican can homestead there. And when a man has land, then he has self-respect and he will be respected. That is the way we want to live, not like this in New York."

My father agreed, adding, "But you cannot blame this country. It has been good for me and many like me."

"I do not blame this country," the Puerto Rican said. "All I say is this. The time of opportunity for poor people from another country is almost gone here. Now, they must find another America."

The loud-speaker called the departure of a plane. This time, the Puerto Ricans listened intently until it was repeated. Then they picked up their handbags and prepared to go. But, before they left, they looked at us almost shyly, and one of them, the one who had been doing most of the talking, held out his hand to my father. He seemed almost afraid to do so. But my father grasped it firmly, and there was a flash of white teeth in a dark face, and the grateful warmth of black eyes smiling.

"*Con Dios*," my father said.

"And He with you, good friend," the Puerto Ricans said, and then were gone.

In a little while, the last lights of New York were lost in the night, and we were flying out over the black Atlantic. Because of the long delay, it was to be a non-stop flight, and we would not see land again until morning and France.

Now, for the first time, America was really behind us and the trip was consummated. In that moment of departure, a visible change had come over my father. It was more than wheels lifting in good-by from a free land, or the bold lights of an American city fading and growing dim and finally disappearing in the darkness, and, with them, all that America must have meant to a man like him.

What had brought it about was something that happened when we were boarding the Air France plane. In the line in front of us, there was a Frenchman, fat and more than a little pompous, with the irritability of a petty official. Before we mounted the steps, he had paused to tell his impatience in loud and gesturing French to the steward. For an instant, the steward had taken up the argument, but when the line began to crowd, he had shrugged and submitted to the word whipping.

At the top of the steps, the Frenchman had paused again to speak his mind to the stewardess. She apologized with some restraint and ushered the Frenchman past her. He went all the way down the aisle to the front of the plane, but apparently could not find any seat to his liking, and doubled back.

My father was in front of me, and we were just preparing to enter a pair of seats. He even had one foot out of the aisle and into the aperture when the Frenchman came up and indicated by his movements that he wanted that seat. My father drew his foot back with a quickness of motion that was not politeness, but something of deference and almost of fear. The Frenchman took the seat without a word of thanks and with the attitude of one who knows his position.

Later, when the plane took off, my father did not even seem to be aware of it. He turned only once to look out the window at the fading lights of New York. There was an expression on his face of brooding sadness, as though he had suddenly remembered something out of the far past that he had forgotten.

Through the dinner and the tiny bottle of wine that went with it, he spoke very little. Once, the stewardess, who must have recognized him to be an old country man, as the little official had done, asked him gently in French if he were going home. He told her yes, and where we were going, and how long it had been since he had gone away. But when she moved on, he fell silent again with his thoughts.

I think he must have known my anger about the incident. It was not that he had given the Frenchman the seat that bothered me, because he had always done things like that. But before, these acts had been done out of kindness. This time, there was something else in it. He was a man who could not have explained the word pride, and yet wore it with all the natural dignity of a deer in the hills. But in that moment, the pride had faltered, and it had come to me as a bitter surprise.

The flight was not a placid one. We were running into unsettled weather, and the plane was dipping and bumping often. Yet, my father gave no sign of having noticed. After a while, he began to talk about something that had happened when he had left home to come to America, and, in its way, I guess it was an explanation.

"We met him at this little hotel in Paris, where we was supposed to stay for the two nights before we got onto the boat," my father said. "He was a young man, not much older than us, and although he said he was from near our town in the Basque country, we knew from his speech that he was a *manesa*, from down lower in the Pyrenees. And I don't hardly think he was using his right name, because he seemed to forget and not answer to it one time when Jean, my friend, called him.

"He was a nice boy, but awfully quiet. When he spoke in French, it was beautiful to listen to, because it was so perfect. He was pale, which surprised us for someone coming from the Basque country, and we wondered about that too, because he said he happened to be working on the family property when he decided to come to America."

In the plane, the stewardess began to move about with little pillows for the passengers, and my father put his on his lap for the time being.

"All the time we was in Paris," he went on, "Michel, which was his name, stayed always in his room except for when it was time to eat. He wouldn't go out into the streets with us at all, even though we asked him whenever we went. We began to think something pretty bad was wrong, and then one day, the day we was to leave on the boat, something happened that made us sure."

My father was silent for a few moments, and then he said, "I don't know if you've ever seen a brave man afraid. It's a sad thing to see. Oh, I don't mean to be afraid like in a fight, because there you at least have a chance. There's worse ways to be afraid than that. I mean to be afraid of the government. To do courageous things you knew was right, and yet they was wrong because the government said so. Not to have the right to speak your own tongue in the schools or anywhere, for one thing, even though it was a tongue that was older than the French by far. And, by that more than anything else, to be made to feel that it was a crime to be born a Basque."

There was a white anger in my father's face that I had seen few times in my life. He shook his head violently to clear his mind.

"It was the day we was to leave on the boat for America," he said, "and we had all gotten up early to eat our breakfast downstairs. While we was eating, a gendarme came into the hotel. I was sitting next to Michel, and when we saw the gendarme I felt his legs go like iron under the table. The gendarme looked at us, and then he went to where the proprietor was, and we could hear him ask if there was any Basques in the hotel that was going to America. And, without turning around, we knew that the proprietor had pointed to us, and that the gendarme was coming over to our table."

In the plane, the stewardess dimmed the lights, and seats began to lower as the passengers made themselves comfortable for the night.

"Michel was trying to act like everything was all right," my father went on, "but he couldn't hold his spoon steady in the bowl, and the gendarme seen it because I saw his eyes go to his hands and then to his face. He stood above our table and asked us for our papers, first mine and then Jean's. And when he looked at them, he asked questions in French about where we was from, and our names, and why we was going. But he seemed most of all to be listening to the way we spoke. And when he was through with us, his voice changed like he was talking to a criminal, and he asked Michel for his papers.

"Michel's face was white as a ghost, and when he handed his papers to the gendarme his fingers was shaking. The gendarme looked at the papers and then asked him a question in that same voice. Michel tried to speak, but his throat must of been awful, because he couldn't bring the words out."

The plane dipped suddenly into an air pocket, and a few passengers raised their heads in alarm, then after a moment relaxed on their pillows.

"The gendarme asked him again," my father said. "But before Michel could answer, my friend Jean spoke up quickly. He told Michel in Basque, so that the gendarme could not understand, not to say one word in French. Then Jean turned to the gendarme and began talking like a fool. He said that Michel couldn't speak French hardly at all, because he had been sick for many years and could not go to school, and so he spoke only

Basque, and that was why he was so pale, and that he was sickly, and not very smart either. And he said it so that it seemed to be a joke between him and the gendarme. And before the gendarme could answer, Jean went off on a long story about all the stupid things Michel had done in the Basque country, and how it was the laugh of the town, and how his family hoped that he would get better and maybe a little smarter in America."

My father smiled almost sadly, and said, "The gendarme tried to say something a few times, but he couldn't stop Jean from talking, and finally he threw up his arms and went out of the hotel. After he was gone, and we went upstairs to get our things, Michel got sick to the stomach."

"But didn't you ever find out what was wrong?" I asked.

My father nodded. "Yes," he said, "but not until we was almost ready to land in New York, although we suspected what it was. One night, when we was outside watching the ocean, Michel told us. He had thought he wanted to be a priest, so he went to the French seminary. But after he was there a while, he knew that the life wasn't for him. Just before he was to be ordained, he ran away. He hid in the Basque country while his family arranged for his papers to come to America."

"But I don't understand," I said. "Why should he have to run away?"

"Because he would of been thrown in jail if he didn't," my father said. And, seeing my amazement, he added, "I don't think you can understand what it is to live with laws like that. In America, you have grown

78

up with a government you can cuss and argue with and fight, and win just as often as you lose." He shrugged "And I guess maybe it's the same way in France now, too. It's funny," he mused, "it's so easy to get used to living with a government like that. I know, because I had forgotten how it was too." And, after a while, he said, "But I won't forget again."

9

Since the first light of day, we had been flying high over an expanse of clouds and mist that stretched as far as the eye could see in every direction. It was late morning when the stewardess announced that we were coming into Paris. My father grinned at me self-consciously, and he could not conceal the excitement in his eyes.

The plane began to descend, and after a moment we could catch glimpses of green fields through the thinning clouds. Then suddenly, like a curtain parting, the clouds broke away and the great, flat plains of France were before us. Outlying farms and buildings and the Seine River and the Eiffel Tower moved in succession past our little window. The plane banked steeply and then leveled off as it came in for a landing. Our wheels touched ground and we were on the soil of France.

"Well, I'll be durned," my father said. "You know, I never thought we'd make it."

In the hours of confusion that followed, beginning with customs and the autobus ride into Paris and ending with the Air France announcement that our plane to Bordeaux would not be leaving until the next morning, and we would have to spend the night in Paris—he remained miraculously detached from it. He could not see enough of what was happening around him, but devoured it all in silence.

We were to stay at a hotel with which Air France had made arrangements, and by the time we finished our business and arrived there it was late afternoon. While our bags were being carried in, we went to the desk in the lobby to register. The clerk was a tall, serious-looking man in a dark suit.

My father and I were both leaning against the desk. We had finished registering and were almost ready to go when the clerk looked up without warning and said to my father, *"Eskualduna?"*

My father jumped as though he'd been prodded with a needle. He regarded the clerk for an instant, and then nodded his head and answered, *"Bai. Eskualduna naiz."*

"I thought so," said the clerk in Basque. "I have never made a mistake yet."

"But what are you doing here?" my father said incredulously.

"I hold the position here," said the clerk.

"I can see that," my father said. "But what I mean is how did you get here?"

"Oh," said the clerk, divining my father's question, "I believe I know what you mean. You must have been away for a long time. There are many Basques in Paris now." He looked at our registration. "You have been in

America, I see. How many years since you have seen France?"

"Forty-seven years," my father said.

"*Zer gauza!*" the clerk whistled. "And you are going to the Basque country, naturally. What is your town?"

"Tardets," my father said.

"You are a *zhibero*, eh?" the clerk said. "I thought so. Tell me, do you have any people there?"

My father hesitated strangely before he answered. "Yes. Four sisters still living, there and nearby."

The clerk shook his head. "They will be excited to see you," he said. "They know you are coming, of course."

"I wrote them that I was," my father said. "But I don't think they will believe it until I am there."

"That is true," the clerk said. "I remember when I was a boy, we had two uncles in America who were always coming back the next year. And my mother kept the property shining and our best clothes put away for the time when they would. But they finally died before they came." He clucked his tongue. "It was a shame. I wore that suit only once before I grew out of it."

"Has everything changed there as much as here in Paris?" my father asked.

The clerk shook his head. "In the mountain properties, nothing seems to change very much. But there is some difference in the villages. Many of the roads are paved, and some of the people have cars. And of course there is electricity now, at least in the villages."

"Well, I'll be durned," my father said in English.

"What did you say?" the clerk said.

"Nothing," my father said. "I was wondering if I

could send a telegram to my people."

"Well, of course," the clerk said.

"I will then, tomorrow before we leave for Bordeaux," my father said. He held out his hand to the clerk. "We will see you again before we leave."

"Good," the clerk said, shaking his hand. "If you don't mind my saying it, I think you should not forget to send the telegram. Otherwise, it might be too much of a shock for them, especially if they are old."

My father nodded, and the strange hesitation repeated itself. "They are old, all right," he said.

Later, in our room, he sat on the edge of the bed and stared at the floor for a long time. He seemed to be trying to settle something in his mind. Finally, he said, "How different it is. Where before there was buggies and horses and long dresses, now, there's cars and airplanes and the same kind of clothes you see in America. It seems that in your memory of things you knew a long time ago, it stays the same and nothing ever changes. You say to yourself, 'Well, things have changed there too, you know,' but you can't hardly believe it until you see it with your own eyes."

He was silent for a moment, and then he said slowly, "And yet, inside, you don't change at all. I feel right now the same kind of excitement I felt when we was getting ready to go on the boat. And somewhere far inside, I catch myself thinking that I'm still a boy, that I'm no older than I was when I left. Then I catch a look at my hands, and I realize that that's changed too, that now I'm an old man. And I think of going home, and again I catch myself thinking of my brothers and my sisters and Mamma and Papa as they was when I left, and that they will be waiting at home for me. And it comes to me that the only ones who are left are my sisters, and even they must be old by now, and the rest are all gone, and I can never see them again."

It was night and dinner was done, and, after all, we were in Paris. So we did as the Frenchmen did, and walked slowly along the Champs-Elysées, stopping often to look in through the high, lighted windows of the stores.

My father could not get over it. He marveled at the gleaming little cars on display, the richness of the furs on the manikins, and even the fine leather that went into the shoes. And when we came to our first theater and saw that an American movie was playing there, he was amazed. For an instant, he argued that we should go see it, until I convinced him that this would be a sacrilege when there were only a few hours to be spent in Paris.

And so we ventured out on the avenue and crossed at risk of life and limb to the Arc de Triomphe, arriving there with my father's mutterings that the French drivers must be blind or crazy, or both. Beneath the towering stone arch, he told me of how his grandfather had been to Paris once, in a revolution, and how he told afterward with shakings of his head how men had gone crazy with the smell of blood, and how that blood ran red in the streets. Still, his grandfather had spoken of at least the journey in pride, because, after all, there were few Basques in that day who had even seen Paris.

We strolled far up the avenue until the darkened side streets of Paris began to press against the lighted way.

Tired from walking, we sat down in a sidewalk café and watched the night people disappear into the shadows. My father had a grin on his face.

"You know," he said, "I can't tell for sure, but it seems to me that this must be the same café where Jean and I happened to be sitting one night while we was waiting to go to America. It's just about the same place, because I remember there wasn't too many lights here then either." He shook his head and whistled. "Jesus crackers! What a night that was."

"Well, what happened?" I said.

"Are you sure you'll never tell your mother?" he said.

"I wouldn't do that, Pop," I said.

"Well, I'll tell you then," he said. "But you better be sure."

"I'm sure, Pop," I said.

"Well, you know," he began, "I don't know how to say it. It sounds a little funny." He shrugged his shoulders and sighed. "But anyway, we'd gotten tired from walking around, and so here we was sitting to have a little rest and a drink of wine and to watch the people going by. I don't know where they came from, but all of a sudden there was two ladies standing by our table. They had on long dresses like they wore in those days, and big fancy hats, and they smelled of perfume so much it made you a little dizzy.

"At first, when they just stood there looking at us, we thought maybe we had their table or something, and so we got up. But then, one of them said, 'Good evening. May we join you?'

"Well, of course we said yes," my father explained. "What else could we do, you tell me. We didn't know who they was, but we both thought to ourselves that this must be the way they did things in Paris. Although I remember wondering why nobody ever told us about people being so nice and friendly in the city.

"They both sat down right away, moving their chairs so that one of them was close to Jean and the other close to me. And the funny thing about it was that no sooner was they sat down, than they both at the same time put their hands to their chests and said, 'Oh, I'm so thirsty.' "

My father squirmed uncomfortably. His ears had reddened considerably since he began talking. "So there we was with nothing we could do but ask them to have a little drink for their thirst. I don't know what they ordered, but it sure cost enough. And I noticed that when the waiter served it, he had a sort of laugh on his face, and that made me wonder a little bit, but not very much right then.

" 'You are not from Paris,' the one whose name was Mlle Nanette said.

" 'Oh no,' said Jean. 'We are from the Basque country.'

" 'We thought so!' the other lady whose name I can't remember said. 'We could tell by your strength.' And she reached over and felt Jean's arm with her fingers, and he looked at me with a pretty durned foolish smile.

" 'And what are you doing in Paris?' Mlle Nanette asked.

" 'We are going to America,' I explained. 'Our boat leaves very soon.' And the other lady, who was always getting excited, put her hand to her neck and said, "Ooo! You must have money then.' "

My father looked stern for an instant. "Well, that seemed to me a pretty funny thing to say," he said. "But that *ergela* Jean must not of thought so, because he puffed up a little and patted his pocket and said, 'Oh yes, naturally we have money.'

"The other lady made one of those noises again and said right away, 'Let me see it!' "

My father made a tching sound and continued to look stern. "I don't know if that Jean would of actually showed it to her," he said. "But sometimes I wonder. Anyway, before he could, this gendarme came walking by. And right then, I noticed that Mlle Nanette happened to reach under the table and tap the other lady on the knee. The gendarme stopped in the street and looked for a minute like he was going to come over to the table, but then he turned around and walked away. And right then," my father said, "I began to get a little suspicious."

He paused and took a sip of his drink. The stern expression gave way, and he slunk down slightly in his chair.

"Well," he went on, "those ladies didn't say hardly a word until the gendarme was gone. They both finished their drinks just like that. Mlle Nanette put her hand to her mouth to cover a yawn, and she said, 'Oh, I am so tired.' And then she said, 'Could we ask you gentlemen to walk with us to our hotel? Just as protection for ladies, you know.' "

My father cleared his throat. By now, his ears were flaming red. "Well, of course we had to say yes," he said. "What else could we do, you tell me. We didn't know anything except that they was ladies and they shouldn't be allowed to walk home alone at night.

"So, we got up and right away Mlle Nanette took ahold of my arm, and the other one did the same thing to Jean, and we started walking. We had only gone a little way, and it was getting darker, when I heard the other one say to Jean, 'You must be tired, too. Would you like to come to my room and have a little rest?'

"Jean had been laughing in that foolish way. But when she said that, he stopped pretty durned quick. And right then, Mlle Nanette spoke to the other one real sharp and low, and I think part of what she said was, 'Too soon!'"

By now, my father was in a state of excitement. He took a big swallow of his drink and squirmed again in his chair. "I'm telling you," he said. "We knew something was wrong, and we both stopped walking at the same time. Just then, a little man in a suit came out of one of those dark streets and happened to say something not very nice to those two ladies we were with, and kept right on walking. What he said was bad enough, but you should have heard what Mlle Nanette said back to him. Whew!

"When she said what she did, both Jean and I pulled loose from them and backed a little away. 'Where are you going, little one?' the other lady said, real sweet.

" 'I think I forgot my beret at the café,' that foolish Jean said, when all the time it was sitting on his head.

" 'Oh no, you didn't,' Mlle Nanette said, and they both took a step after us.

" 'Oh yes, I did,' said Jean, and when we backed up again, they came after us, still arguing about that silly beret. Until, finally, there we was backing up like hell

88

and they after us. Then, they started to run to catch us, and I'm telling you it was close. We turned around and just made it off, running like fools. And we could hear them for a long time, screaming at us, and they sure wasn't talking very sweet then."

"Did you get away?" I asked.

My father looked offended. "Of course we got away," he said. "We ran all the way back to the hotel and got up in our room and locked the door before we ever stopped." He finished his drink and took a deep, exhausted breath. "What a night!" he said. "I hope that never happens again."

"Well, I don't know," I said. "I just saw a lady walk by and look at you. From her expression, I thought maybe she knew you from somewhere."

My father looked around wildly. Then it dawned on him and he shook his head in mild reprimand. "You shouldn't pull a joke like that," he said. "What happened that night was a pretty serious thing, you know."

"I'm sorry, Pop," I said, but, try as I might, I could not keep a straight face.

ฅฦฅฦฅฦฅฦฅฦฅฦฅฦฅ *10*

He might as well not have been married thirty years at all. In the eyes of my mother's Bordeaux relatives he was still a young swain seeking approval for her hand in marriage.

My father had never known my mother in the old country. Although she too was Basque, she had been raised in the low, gentle hills of the Pyrenees and in Bordeaux, where her family had a travel business. However, it was an old family whose position of authority among the lowland Basques dated back to the time of the Romans, and he had of course heard of them when he was young, much like the country boy in an American town who has heard with no little awe of the family that lives in the big white house on the hill.

Besides that, he had still another obstacle to overcome. My father was a *zhibero,* and the young girls of my mother's province had been reared to be wary of these wild and foolish boys of the high Pyrenees. And though now in meeting the family, he was in truth old, he was still one of those *zhibero* boys, therefore to be regarded with caution.

My mother's family in Bordeaux now consisted of two sisters, Claire and Aurelie. Claire, who was dark-haired and plump, was married and had three young children. Her husband Maurice, a tall man who wore a scholarly pince-nez and yet had a jovial Basque air about him, now headed the family's travel business. He had been a French army officer in the second World War and had had his leg blown off when the Maginot line fell, but he ignored this handicap and moved about with amazing vigor. My mother's other sister, Aurelie, who was fair-haired and beautiful, had never married, and so she too lived with the family.

After a cursory inspection, they seemed to take me for granted and accepted me into the family readily. After all, I was of their blood too, so naturally I had to be acceptable. But my father couldn't get off that easily. He was an outsider, and he had to prove himself.

I don't know whether they expected him to break momentarily into a wild *zhibero* dance on a wineglass or give a western cowboy whoop such as they had heard in the movies, but their attitude at the beginning was one of some apprehension. When my father in spite of his rugged appearance acted at all times like a gentleman, they began to warm to him, nodding their heads approvingly at his good command of French, his ability as a storyteller, and his lively if at times shocking sense of humor. Of course, his trim appearance in the new suit which he had now taken to wearing helped more than a little.

Dinner that first night was a festive occasion. The table had been set with the family silver and crystal, and the linen napkins were the special ones that bore the old family insignia. There were *apéritifs* before dinner, and for the first time the conversations began to break away from the impersonal French and lapse occasionally into the familiar Basque.

The first time my father spoke in Basque, though, Maurice regarded him curiously. He leaned forward listening until my father finished, and then said incredulously, "Dominique, unless I am mistaken, you don't talk too much like a *zhibero*. You talk almost like us, like a *manesa*."

My father was a little taken aback. He had obviously not been aware of it himself. He thought about it for a minute, and then said solemnly, "Well, that could mean only one thing. Since I got married, I've been doing most of the listening."

Maurice laughed uproariously and slapped his leg, and even my mother's sister, Claire, could not resist a tiny grin.

After that, the family began asking the first real questions about my mother and home, as if what they had asked before had been only the proper questions, and what he had answered had been the same. "How is she, Dominique?" said Aurelie simply.

"As well as you could expect," my father said. "She's still a pretty woman, but a little old, and a little gray like the rest of us, and a little tired now that the family's raised. It wasn't easy for her."

"She never complained in her letters," said Aurelie. "but I could tell." She paused for an instant, and a disappointment that had been there before returned to her eyes. "Why did she not come back with you, Dominique?"

My father's brow furrowed. "I'm not sure about it," he began. "She said that except for you two sisters, and maybe a few of her cousins, she had no great wish to see France again." He stopped and thought about it for a while. "Somehow, she's afraid of something. I think it's the trip, and I can understand that, because I was too, you know. But after all how much of a trip is it now? A few days ago, we were in Nevada, and now," and he clapped his palms together, "poof! Here we are in Bordeaux. You wouldn't believe it." He raised his hands helplessly as he tried to put it together again. "But maybe it isn't the trip at that." He spoke slowly. "I think she's afraid something will happen to her here, away from her children, and that she'll never see them again. And you know how she feels about her children. She wants to be where she can see them and help them if there's any trouble." He laughed a little. "But, there again, it's a funny thing. Now that the children are grown up, they feel that she had enough worry, and they don't want to tell her if they have any troubles. They go to each other, but they don't tell us until it's all over."

"She was like that from the beginning," said Aurelie. "She was the oldest of us, you know, and she worried over us as though we were her children. When our brother, Michel, went to America and became sick, as we had dreaded he would, she was the one to insist that she would go to him." Even after thirty years, her lip trembled as she said, "It was to be such a short trip. I remember when we went to the boat with her, and when we said good-by, she said she would bring us souvenirs of America. Who would have dreamed that day that neither of them would ever come back, and we would never be together again?"

"But you must know that she tried to bring him back," my father said. "It was that he wouldn't hear of it, even though he knew he would die."

Claire nodded her head severely. "I knew it. I suspected it and I knew it. In her letters, she said that he was already too sick to make the trip, but I knew what the reason was. Michel was proud as our father was proud, and neither would bend to the other, not even in death. And our sister, your wife, knew that better than anyone else. I remember when she was to leave, she went to Papa and said, 'You must give me leave to say that you have asked him to come home to us.' But Papa, even though in his heart he wanted it more than anything in the world, said to her, 'Never!' And she said, 'You must, or you will not see him again.' And Papa began to cry in his eyes alone, but again he said, 'Never!'"

"I don't know how much our sister has told you," Aurelie said to my father, "but the trouble began in the war. It was so hard for Papa to see him go. Because Michel was educated, however, he was given a post in an office far back of the lines. When that happened, Papa was happy. But after a few months, when word was coming back of his friends dying in battle, Michel could not bear it any longer. I remember the day when he came home. He was so straight and tall and beautiful in his uniform, and stood before Papa and said, 'I have asked to go to the front.' For a moment, I thought **Papa** would die of the hurt and the fear. But he stood to **face** Michel and he said, 'Go, then! And, from this minute, you are dead and I have no son!' And Michel went to the front with his friends, and of course you know how he was caught in the battle by the poison gas of the Germans. Even when the war was over, and they sent him home from the hospital, Papa would not speak to him, and that was why Michel ran away to America.''

My father frowned, and said hesitantly, ''I don't know if I should tell you this, because I don't think my wife has written it to you. But enough time has passed that you should know. When your sister and I first met, it was in Reno, where Michel was in the hospital. For a time, it seemed that he would get well. He was so happy, but I think it was because he knew that Theresa would not be alone in America after he was gone. Then one day, when we had almost begun to hope that a miracle had happened and he would get well, the beginning of the end came and the doctors told us that he was dying. I remember the poor boy, lying in his bed and not much left of him then, with the holy candles burning around his bed and the nuns praying on their knees. It happened when we were not even sure he was breathing. His eyes opened suddenly, and he raised himself in bed and he said 'Shhh!' in a command, as if he were hearing something that we could not hear. I was beside him, and I tried to make him lie down again, but he grabbed my arm with a terrible grip, and he whispered, 'Listen! My father's footsteps! Can't you hear them?' And he began to cry with happiness, but only for a minute. And then he turned to me, his eyes on fire, and he cried,

'He's behind the door now! He wants to come in! But I will not see him! Tell him I will not see him!' Then he fell back on the bed, and he did not open his eyes again. And in a little while, he died."

In the silence that followed, there was a moan of anguish from Aurelie. When she could speak again, she cried bitterly, "The pride of the Basques. I think it is to their shame, shame, shame!"

For a man like my father, who loved the taste of wine, it must have been a treat. This was wine country, and there had been a different kind with every course, from the soup to the oysters to the steak, served in a succession of heavy crystal glasses. When dessert came, Maurice had gone down to the wine cellar and brought back a bottle of champagne so old that he had to wipe the cobwebs from it.

When dinner was done and the maid had long since cleared the table, we sat with coffee and brandy late into the night while my father told them of Michel's funeral, and how the American Legion had fired a volley over his grave, and where the grave was, and what kind of a stone it had, and how my mother went every Decoration Day to put flowers on it.

"But it's a funny thing," he said. "He doesn't belong there dead any more than he did alive. He didn't know the land and the land didn't know him, and his grave is like a stranger to it."

Afterward, my father told them of the wedding. As Basques went, there had been a lot of them in western Nevada then, and they had come in full force to the wedding. He had been rich, and they had done the affair up in fine style. My mother was young and slender and beautiful in her lace wedding dress, and my father had a new suit and, in honor of the occasion, had shaved off the black handlebar mustache he had so recently grown. There had been many flowers, and, after the ceremony, a banquet and music and dancing in the old country way.

It had been a good life for a while, anyway. They had lived in a big, two-story white house on the ranch that was the headquarters for the spread. And though she had kept busy with duties like arranging meals for all the herders and buckaroos and handymen and even supervising the dressing of the hogs for hams and bacon and sausage, she had found time to embroider and read and take long walks in the autumn sun, and plan for the arrival of her first child.

As he talked, I thought of the things that he could not say. About how she had been so busy and happy that she did not even suspect something had gone terribly wrong. And yet, later, she could remember little things that should have told her what was happening.

There were the days when my father did not laugh as much as he used to, and nights when he began to toss in his sleep. She had asked him what was wrong, and he had said something about a band of sheep being sick from bad feed, and she had let it go at that, because that was a man's business, even though she had wondered a little how something so usual could bother him so much.

There were the days when my father ceased laughing altogether, and when he rode his horse out of the yard in the early dawn, he was gaunt and grim and too straight in the saddle.

And then there was the time when he dressed up and went alone to Reno in the big, black Cadillac. When he came home that night, it was late and she was asleep. The sound of voices in the room downstairs awakened her finally, and she lay listening sleepily for a while before she realized that it was the partners and foremen, and that there was an argument going on. Even then, though she came wide awake, she did not leave her bed until suddenly the argument stopped and voices grew taut and slow and frightening. Then she had slipped on her robe and gone quickly out of the room and to the head of the stairs.

They had looked up at her then, and straightened and quit talking. One of the partners took off his hat and said hello to her in a nice but strained voice, and that had broken the menace in the room. They all said good night and left the house. My father went outside with them, and in a little while he came back in. His eyes were sick and blazing, and his face was so white he looked as if he were dead. In the darkness of the bedroom, he sat on the edge of the bed and told her that the bottom had fallen out of the market, that they were losing the cattle to the bank, and maybe even the ranch itself, and if they were lucky they might save some of the sheep.

In the middle of telling her, his voice grew strange, as if he were listening to his own words and, hearing them, realizing for the first time the nightmare that was happening. She spoke to him, but he did not answer. He got up and went to the door and half turned there as though he were thinking of something, and then went out.

In a little while, she followed him. The big room downstairs was dark, and he was sitting in front of the fire. She spoke to him again, but this time he did not hear her. In terror, she saw the light glinting from the carbine that was propped near the fireplace. It was where it always was, but now it had a meaning.

Through the long hours of the night, she lay stiff with dread in the upstairs bedroom, clutching her rosary and saying over and over again, "Give him the strength to live this night through."

With the first light of morning, she heard his footsteps on the stairs. He came in and, thinking that she was asleep, changed quietly into his work clothes and went out again. The night had passed.

"Of course," my father said, "we weren't the only ones who were bad off in those days. Some of the biggest men there were in livestock had nothing left, and I used to see so many of them going like me from one camp to another, wherever there was work, herding sheep or buckarooing like they had done in the beginning. But some of them had gotten a little old, and it hurt you to see them hiking after the sheep or getting on a spooky horse in the cold mornings."

"And Theresa went with you to these camps?" asked Aurelie a little incredulously.

My father lifted his hands. "What else was there to do? The children were still coming, and we both of us had to work to make enough to stay alive. Whenever her time would come, she would go to a town to be near a doctor, but when it was over she would come back to the camps again. She would do the cooking for the men, sometimes thirty or forty of them, three times a day, on the big ranches that hadn't gone under."

"And still take care of her children?" said Claire.

"Of course," my father said, regarding her as though he wondered who else she thought had taken care of the children. "It meant a lot of work, all right, but she was strong and she never seemed to mind it. What was hard on her was living in the tents. She never took to that at all. She wanted walls around her, even if it was only a cabin." He looked at the table and thought for a moment. "Still, it took some courage all right."

He was right about that. It took courage all right for a woman to live in the sheep camps. And it took courage not to keep on living that way, to make her own opportunity and come to Carson City as she did, out of an old brown-board cabin in the desert, with four children and a hundred dollars, to start another life in the little hotel, doing all the cooking and serving for the working-men boarders, and taking care of their rooms, on her feet from four o'clock in the morning until midnight, and with only half enough sleep at night. And it took courage for a pretty woman to watch slender legs become a mass of purple veins forever from standing on her feet until the last day of the ninth month, and then deliver her child and go back to work.

Even after we had left the hotel and my father had gone back to the hills with his sheep, it took courage to face a life with six children who could have gone one way or another, and do it with an iron rule, without fear ever once showing, and with a love that was there in little things like a touch of the hand or an unguarded glance, because if she had ever shown fear or weakness or too much love, she would have been lost.

It took courage all right, but it took something else too. It had to do with forty mornings of Lent, up when the sky was still dark and the snow was piled high on the ground, trudging a narrow path to the church, with her brood strung out behind her, little dark patches moving slowly through the white snow, huddled deep in their coats, shivering, and with eyes still stuck with sleep.

It had to do with winter nights when the big trees outside the house moaned fearfully with blizzards, and long after the children had gone to bed a single candle burned in the living room, and a wife prayed for her husband in the hills.

11

Somewhere in the darkness beyond loomed the beginning of the Pyrenees, and high in those mountains the home of my father. We were in the foothills of the Basque country, but night had fallen and everything about us was lost in obscurity.

Yet, as fleeting as glimpses out of memory, scenes that told us where we were, caught and hung momentarily in the passing headlights of our car, and then were gone in the darkness. There was a little boy in a beret and short trousers, and under his arm a loaf of bread that seemed as long as he was. There was a crude, wooden cart pulled by two oxen, whose nodding heads kept rhythm with the gay fringes on their horns. There was a girl in a scarf and bright peasant dress, visiting with her young man at the juncture of a country lane, whose eyes our lights brushed in passing, and whose laughter tinkled after us in the night like tiny bells.

And, once, we stopped the car by the side of the road

to watch the men coming home from the fields. The air was sweet with the smell of new-cut hay, and the call of the night birds came softly to our ears. The working-men trudged like shades in single file through the darkness, their wooden shoes clacking hollow on the cobblestones, and the song they sang was the low, mournful song of the close of day. *"Gaihun,"* said my father as they passed by the car, and an old voice said gently back, *"Gaihun."*

When they were gone, and we could not see or hear any more, Maurice put a hand on my father's shoulder and said, "What are you thinking, old shepherd?"

My father did not answer for a while, and then he said, quietly and with difficulty, "How well I remember the sound of the shoes and the shadow of the scythe aginst the night. When I was a little boy and I would hear the clacking of the wooden shoes, I would run out into the dark and meet my father at the road, and say, 'Good evening, my father,' and he would take my hand in his, with fingers so hard and bent, and we would walk together to the house."

"It's a good memory," said Maurice.

Before we got into the car, my father paused for a moment to look ahead in the direction of the high Pyrenees. "Tomorrow," said Maurice. "We should be there by tomorrow."

A little farther up the cobblestone road, we stopped at the inn where we were to spend the night. It was a Basque inn with polished oak floors so worn that the knots showed, and oaken beams overhead, and an old fireplace that was used for cooking no more, but with its massive copper andirons and utensils clean and gleaming and still in place.

The proprietor, an old friend of Maurice's, met us at the door in a big white apron. He was a Basque with a round face and happy eyes suffused in fat, and he smiled with the quiet good humor of a wise man.

"An old countryman," Maurice said as he introduced my father. "An old countryman come home."

The proprietor nodded as if he had known it from the first glance. He looked at my father and asked, "How many years?"

"Forty-seven," my father said. "Forty-seven years."

The proprietor nodded again, but did not say anything. He ushered us into the hallway, where we washed our hands in a basin and dried them on a common wayfarers' towel. Then we sat down to a dinner of soup and omelette with wine and bread. It was served by a pretty Basque girl with black eyes and thick auburn hair pulled back and caught at the nape of her neck. Her skin, which looked as if it had never known make-up, glowed with the robust good health of a country girl. Serving us dinner must have been a doubtful pleasure, because Maurice, who knew of the romance, teased her continuously about the proprietor's son, so that she was in a constant blush.

As we were eating dinner, the proprietor came out from the kitchen every once in a while to visit. Once, he brought his son out to meet us. He resembled his father, but in a young and sturdier cast, with his serious bent of mind showing and not concealed, like his father's. The only time his composure broke a little was when Maurice joshed him about the household romance, and he grinned quickly and almost blushed too, before he caught himself.

When dinner was over, the proprietor came and sat down at the table and had wine with us. He looked at my father often, as though he were considering him and had something on his mind he wanted to talk about. After a while, when the little barriers were down, he brought it up.

"Do you know Wyoming?" he asked.

My father was a little taken aback. "Just what I have heard about it from the *Eskualdunac* who were there," he said. "Why do you ask?"

"I was there myself once, many years ago," the proprietor said. "I herded sheep for two years. I went only to make money," he said frankly, "and after I had made it, I came back and bought this inn, as I had planned."

"I wouldn't have known from talking to you that you were ever in America," my father said. "You don't even have any of the cuss words in your talking. Did you learn English at all?"

The proprietor shrugged. "*Kazu.* When one is a herder in the hills," he said slyly, "there is very little English that he can learn from his jackass."

Though it was another twist on a retort that he had heard before, it still brought a laugh to my father's lips and an appreciative guffaw from Maurice. The proprietor joined quietly in the laughter, making no sound, but the whole of his round body shaking with mirth. "I am sorry," he chuckled. "I did not mean to make a joke." His laughter subsided, and he said, "It is strange, but I had not even the slightest desire to learn English.

105

All I wanted was to make the money and come back to my own country."

"Well," my father said, "I think that in the beginning that was why we all went. But it seems like things happened and we never could come back."

"I wonder," the proprietor said. "There was once when I believed that it was only circumstances, either good or bad, that kept them there. But often since then I have wondered." He paused and said earnestly to my father, "Tell me, were there not times in your life when you could easily have come back with all the money you would ever need in the Basque country?"

"Well, not easily," my father began. "When a man has a business, it's not an easy thing to give it up."

"But if you had a business," the proprietor said, "then you probably had more money than you had ever thought you would make in the first place. And if coming back to the Basque country was what you wanted more than anything else, would you not have sold the business and come back?"

"But it's not an easy thing to sell a business," my father persisted evasively.

"But it can be done," the proprietor said.

"*Debria!* Of course it can be done," my father said exasperatedly. "But—" he began.

The proprietor waved his hands. "That's what I mean," he said. "And that is what began to make me think why so many who said they wanted to come back always had an excuse." He made a dismissing gesture with one hand. "Oh, I don't mean the poor little ones who wanted to come back and were not strong enough to save their money. I remember them well from my

106

experience in Wyoming. What can you do about them? They were lost souls, and they did not even have the good fortune to be lost in their own hell. They were foreigners when they came and they will always be foreigners. This is their country, and not America." He shook his head pityingly and began again. "What I mean is with those men who could have come back, and, as I said, made excuses why they could not. I wonder if the truth is that they did not want to come back."

"I think it is the only answer," Maurice interrupted emphatically. "And the reason that they would not admit it is that it would be a betrayal to the country of their birth."

"But would it be a betrayal?" the innkeeper said. "Is it not possible that, even at that early time in these men's lives, things had happened to make them change their minds about the country they wanted, and that their obligation to the old country and their fathers and their families and the fact that they had old country faces and old country accent in their speech were not important after all?"

It was a conversation the likes of which I was sure my father had never heard before. Throughout most of it, he had sat quietly listening as if it had no bearing on him at all. But now, the deep frown lines were in his forehead.

Maurice turned to him. "Well, old countryman, if there is an answer, you should know it."

My father held up his hands defensively. "I don't know it," he said with a grin. "You're making my head hurt with all this deep talk."

"Well, what made you change your mind about

coming back?" Maurice insisted.

"Until I listened to you," my father said, "I didn't know I had ever thought about changing my mind without myself knowing it. But," and he shrugged, "maybe I did. Those things are funny, I guess." The frown lines came back and he gestured to the inn-keeper. "What you said about something happening early to make a man change his mind. I don't know if it changed my mind, but I remember a thing that happened that made me begin to feel different about America, and I couldn't figure out why then and I can't now. But it happened anyway, and I remember it."

My father's head was bent a little, and with one leathered hand he began rubbing a knot in the old wood of the table. "It happened when I was new in America and they sent me into the deserts to herd sheep. You would have to see that country to believe it, but it was so big that even from the top of the highest hill I couldn't see a town or a house, except one little cabin and a corral that were hidden in this gully far below where I had the sheep."

He shook his head and sighed. "Oh, how cruel a country that was. It wasn't like the Pyrenees, where the feed was rich and even when I was twelve years old I could herd the sheep without much trouble. There, for as far as you could see, there was sagebrush and rocks, and the only trees were runted little junipers. Herding in that country was something I never dreamed could be. There was so little feed that the sheep would wake up before daylight and never stop until it was dark, and it was all even a young man could do to keep up with them. If I didn't have the dog, I couldn't have

108

done it. And what dogs they had there then. They were so tough you wouldn't believe it, with strong legs and feet like leather, even though sometimes after a couple of days on the hillsides where it was rocky I would have to wrap my dog's feet in burlap to keep them from bleeding. Those slopes with the rocks were something, even for a man. A pair of boots wouldn't last you two weeks, they would be so torn up.

"The life and the country made my heart sick, and many was the night I cried myself to sleep for ever having come to America. I would get up in the morning when it was still dark, as soon as I heard the sheep moving, and make my coffee, and I would hate for the day to come so that I would have to look at that terrible land."

He straightened in his chair. "Well, anyway, about the cabin," he said. "When they first took me to that range, I used to see a few men walking around down where the cabin was. There were steers and sometimes horses in the corral. Then, after a few days, the men would move the stock out and go north toward the Oregon and Idaho borders, and be gone for a few weeks.

"I asked the camptender once if he knew who they were, and he told me it was an outlaw bunch who rustled cattle and horses, and the leader's name was George Davis, and not to ever get in an argument with them, because they were dangerous men. He said that they would probably come up to the camp once in a while and ask for some meat for a change of diet, and to give it to them."

The innkeeper had filled up the wineglasses, and my father took a long swallow. "Well, one day," he went on, "a couple of them came up to my camp at lunch-time, and one of them I could tell was their leader, George Davis, because he had the limp the camptender had told me about. I couldn't talk hardly any English then, but they could talk a few words of Spanish, so I could understand they wanted some mutton. I picked out a nice yearling and showed it to them, and they were pretty pleased. I cut his throat and hung him up on the juniper to bleed, and while we were waiting we ate the mutton stew I already had on the fire.

"George Davis, the leader, was pretty hard looking, but he seemed to be a nice man. He didn't have a big hat like most of the buckaroos those days, but a regular-sized one with the crown up and rounded, like when you first buy it in the store. But the rest of him, except for a long, black silk scarf he had wrapped around his neck a few times, seemed like it was all leather. He had a leather vest and leather arm cuffs, and leather chaps with wings on them, and beaten-up old spurs. He had a big belt with cartridges in it, and a gun that long. His boots weren't the regular cowboy kind, but were laced boots with high heels, maybe because they were easier on his bad leg, I guess."

My father paused and was silent for a while, and when he went on his voice had a softer note in it. "I didn't notice the other outlaw much at the beginning. He never said anything at all for a long time. He was a young man in his twenties, I guess, but not very far along. He was more of a dandy than Davis was, with a clean shirt and a big black hat that was beginning to look sort of beat up, and he had goat-hair chaps that must have been something to see once. At first, he looked to be pretty mean, so I didn't have much to do with him. But when I was butchering the yearling, he helped out like he knew something about sheep, and I found out that he used to herd, and that he wasn't very mean after all.

"Anyway," my father said, "when they left, Davis told me to come down to the cabin sometime, and I said I would if the sheep were pretty near at noonday, when they stopped to rest. So after a few days, I began to go down once in a while, when I would get a little lonesome, to eat with them and watch them shoot. They used to love to shoot, and you wouldn't believe the things they could do with a pistol. But good God, the money they must have spent on cartridges. I bet what they would shoot up on a day like that would be more than a man would make on wages in a week. And I used to think, no wonder men like that were good with a gun.

"*Bainan,*" and my father nodded his head gravely, "the shooting was what led to my trouble. One day, when I was in the yard watching them shooting at cans to see who could keep one in the air the longest, George Davis and another outlaw, who was one of the roughest-looking men I ever saw, had an argument. They were both awful good with a gun, and they didn't seem to be able to beat each other that day, although George Davis was almost always the best. So they bet quite a bit of money, and they put a gold piece up on the corral fence and backed away, and when I saw it I just didn't believe how any man could hit it."

A grimness came then to my father's face, and the innkeeper, sensing it, leaned a little forward. By this time, the innkeeper's son had finished in the kitchen, and he came to stand with the girl and listen. My father did not seem to be aware that he had an audience.

"Well," he said, "the rough-looking outlaw didn't hit it. He missed with all three shots, even though one time the gold piece looked like it waved a little. He was mad and swearing like the devil, stamping on the ground like he was trying to find something to take it out on. I was standing off from the cowboys a little bit, holding my dog, because he always got scared and would whimper when there was shooting, and the rough-looking one shouted at me, and I remember it exactly, 'Shut that dog up!'

"Right away," my father said, "I bent down and grabbed the dog by the jaws, because I didn't want to cause any trouble, though I didn't see how a little thing like that could bother anybody's shooting. George Davis didn't seem to think so either, because he told me to let the dog go. So I did, and he raised up that long pistol of his and brought it down and knocked that gold piece spinning with the first shot, mind you."

My father stuck his jaw out and jerked his head up and down. "Well, that did it. The rough-looking outlaw blew right up, stamping on the ground and shouting like hell. He turned around and looked at me, and for a second I didn't know what to think. He shouted, 'I told you to keep that dog shut!' and he shot him, right at my feet."

My father let his breath expel slowly, as if he had been keeping it locked in his lungs. "Well, you know," he said, "I went down on my knees to look at the dog, and when I saw his blood pouring out on the ground, the first thing I knew I was crying. I was pretty much of

112

a boy then," he said in apology, "and I guess those things happen when you're young."

He raised his hands helplessly. "The buckaroos didn't do anything, but sort of walked away or went into the cabin. George Davis looked madder than hell, though, but he didn't do anything either, because I guess he didn't want to have trouble in his bunch. He just walked over and picked up the gold piece and leaned against the fence looking at it. And so I took my dog in my arms and carried him up to the camp and buried him."

The innkeeper must have believed that was the end of it, because he had a mystified expression on his face. My father saw it and raised his hand in a gesture that there was more.

"After I buried the dog," he went on, "I began to get a little desperate. The camptender was coming the next day, but I knew it would take him two more days to get another dog back to me from the ranch. And I knew that trying to herd those sheep without a dog would kill me, and that I would lose half of them. Well, that night I rounded them up all right, and it damn near killed me at that. I was sitting by the fire so tired I could barely get any food in my mouth when I heard horses coming up the hill. The first thing that came to my mind was that the rough-looking outlaw was coming back to finish the job, so I went into my tent and got the rifle and came out again. But when the horses got close, I saw who it was.

"It was the young outlaw who had come up to the camp with George Davis that first time, and he was leading a horse with a saddle on him. I couldn't believe it, so I just stood there and didn't say anything. The young outlaw didn't say anything either, but the meanness went out of his face for a second and he sort of grinned like a boy, and then he reined his horse out of the firelight, and I never saw him again, because the whole bunch of them left in a few days.

"Well," my father said, placing both his hands on the table, "even though I knew that horse would last only a few days before getting sorefooted, when I woke up that next morning and saw him there, I can't tell you how I felt, but it was different. I didn't mind seeing the sun come up, and when it did I even felt pretty good about the deserts. For the first time, I didn't feel like a stranger to the land. When I thought about it, I couldn't figure it out, but I knew it sure as hell had something to do with my dog who was dead, and the young outlaw who brought me a horse."

12

Forty-seven years and ten thousand thoughts of home, and here he was where it had all begun. Forty-seven years and ten thousand miles, and he could not bring himself to go the last few steps to home.

This was the country of his birth. The soft, dew-drenched hills of the lowlands had given way to mountains made even more austere by longing shadows, and the villages now were of homes not gaily trimmed in red and green, but of stone, bleak and cold and formidable as fortresses.

These were the people of his beginnings, with the men taller and silent, and in their faces a fierceness bridled close to the surface, as if a long-ago day when Basque warriors strode unconquered was not really so long ago after all.

When we came to Saughis, we were very near my father's town of Tardets. The sun was setting between two high peaks of the Pyrenees, and its last slanting rays were filtering down the slopes and into the town.

There was an old, bereted grandfather with a cane paused in the street to catch the warmth and light of a lingering shaft. He gave no sign of our approach, but regarded us distantly from under shaggy brows. And even when my father spoke, saying in Basque, "Can you tell us the street to the church, *aitatchi?*" the old man stood as though he had heard nothing.

Then, suddenly, he leaned forward and said, incensed, "Don't you know your own country?"

My father flushed a little. "It has been a long time since I have seen this town," he said. "I've been away."

The old man withdrew again as though considering what my father had said. For the first time, I think, he saw that my father was wearing a suit. "Have you seen the world?" he asked.

My father nodded. "A little of it," he said. "I've been to America."

A light came into the old man's eyes. "Dominique?" he said, peering closely into my father's face. He leaned back and said, "Ah! Your nephew the priest said in Mass you were coming back. I remembered you, you know. You were the young one in Tardets who rode so much the horses of the French colonel. I used to watch you from my property. You rode too fast, you know. Everybody said it." He leaned forward again. "But what happened to you? You're an old man."

My father winced and tried to shrug, but could say nothing. Then his eyes widened as recollection came to him and he realized that he knew this bent old grandfather. "Now I remember you!" he exclaimed. "But how is it possible?"

This was the way it was with him. In this first moment of homecoming, all the years in between meant nothing. The day he had left, he was a young man and his sisters were young and his brothers alive, and this was the next day, and he and his sisters were old, and all his brothers were dead, and the forty-seven years in between had not happened. He had left home one day, yesterday, and come home today, and the change was too much for him to bear.

And this was why he could not go home all at once, although he knew that the day was already late and that his sisters awaited him in Tardets. Refusing to give a reason why, he knew also that he must stop in Saughis to visit first with a nephew he had never seen, the son of his brother, but, more than that, the first he was to see of his family, and so temper his homecoming with little realizations.

It was a massive old church with the village dead of generations crowded into the tiny yard beside it, so that the gravestones seemed to be growing in fantastic profusion, some erect and some tipping, and of all sizes, like a garden of stone.

We mounted the steps to the rectory and waited until the housekeeper, an old woman, timidly opened the door. "Is the priest here?" asked Maurice.

"Yes, but he is praying," the housekeeper said, and then, surveying us, "Is it important?"

"We are relatives," my father said.

The housekeeper looked at him and gasped. "I will call the Father," she said. Ushering us into the visiting room, she took her leave, clucking her tongue and almost beside herself with excitement.

Except for a table and chairs and a single crucifix on the wall, the room was bare, and now that day was nearly ended dusk was creeping in the narrow slits of windows. We waited in silence as the housekeeper's footsteps echoed down the hall and faded away. Sitting stiffly on his chair, my father looked about him and said to me, "Think of it! My brother's son a priest. That's a pretty big thing up in this country, you know. It's something to be proud of."

In a moment, footsteps sounded again in the hallway, this time heavier and a little restrained, but still with an urgency of excitement. We rose to our feet as the door swung open and a tall, black-robed figure burst into the room. His features were so unmistakably of family that my father started as though he had seen a ghost.

The priest's gaze searched my father out instantly. He stood looking at him, and then he said, hesitantly, "Uncle?"

My father nodded his head. *"Bai, iloba,"* he said hoarsely in Basque, and the priest went to him in one stride and embraced him with unguarded emotion. He pushed my father to arm's length, and with tears streaming down his face whispered, "I am so honored, my uncle." For a moment, he could not talk, and then he placed a hand on his chest and said, "But why? Why did you come here first?" Then, as realization came to him, he exclaimed, "Ah! But I know!" And he embraced my father with understanding.

We sat at the table in the darkening room while the priest animatedly told my father of how his sisters awaited him even now in Tardets, and that they were in such a terrible state of expectation that they could talk of nothing else, and that Marianne, the one who was so ill in the next village of Montory, was in one way heartbroken because she could not be at the homecoming in Tardets, but also so excited that there was no living with her either.

After we had had wine with him, he hurried us outside. "My aunts will never forgive me if I keep you longer," he said. "And even now," he laughed, "I would be in a terrible position if I were not a priest. I will go in and pray that they will forgive me." Then, seriously, he said, "And, for all we nephews and nieces, to thank God that He has brought our only uncle home to us."

Dusk was giving way to darkness when we came to my father's town. The car slowed as we reached the crest of the hill, and the village lay before us, old and silent, with stone spires and black slate roofs and cobblestone streets. It lay in a little valley cut by hedgerows and slender lines of poplars, and the only sound was the rushing of the black river that coursed down from the peaks above.

The streets were deserted now, and lights burned warm from the homes where the villagers were eating their evening meal. The car moved down the hill and onto the cobblestones that led to the market square. We passed a *plaza* where my father had played handball when he was a boy, and he said, "I thought it was bigger. I wonder if they changed it."

The house of Marie-Jeanne where his sisters were waiting lay on the street that led out of town, and from letters my father thought he knew which one it was. We moved slowly along the street until suddenly he said,

"There, there! There it is. It must be that one!"

There was not a sign of anyone expecting our coming. Maurice stopped the car before the house and my father got out and stood uncertainly in the darkness, putting on his hat and then taking it off. When no one came out of the house, he said, "I'll go see," and moved toward the darkened entrance. He was almost there when the door swung open and he was caught in the full light from inside. A young man poked his head out, took one look at him, and as quickly disappeared, shouting, "He has arrived!"

My father stopped still in his tracks. He hung there in the light, moving neither forward nor back. And slowly out of the doorway they came, three sisters together, to pause wordlessly on the step and stare at him. Then one of them said, in a little sound of recognition that yet pleaded it to be true, "Dominique."

And then he came to them, and they to him, and they were laughing and crying at the same instant, and he was trying to hold them all three at once and call their names and kiss each whitened head in turn, and beyond them the children of the household were shouting and dancing in excitement and coming to him for their embraces, and all along the street doors swung open and neighbors came out on their steps to look and point and call out in ringing voices, "Happiness to you all! May you always be together!"

In the car, when I moved to open the door, Maurice caught me by the arm and said, "Stay. This is his moment, to keep him for all the years of his life. It has nothing to do with you or me."

₂₀₂₀₂₀₂₀₂₀₂₀₂₀₂₀₂₀₂₀ *13*

He was the adventurer who had braved the unknown
land across the sea and found his fortune. He was the
rebel who had broken the bonds of their own longings
and fought the battle and come home victorious. He
was the youth who had gone out into the world in beg-
gar's garb and come back in shining armor.

This was the moment of fulfillment. This was the
moment of reward he could never have known in America. These were the people who had seen him only when
he had set out on his quest, whose vision had not been
dulled by nearness through the long trial, and who now
saw only the shining armor.

In the candlelight from the simple table around
which we sat, their faces shone in adulation and burst-
ing pride. His sisters fussed about him unceasingly,
bringing him little delicacies and filling his wineglass
every time he took a swallow, and asking him again
and again if there were anything he wanted. And

every once in a while, they turned to each other and exclaimed aloud, "How well he looks! How finely he carries himself!"

His protest went in vain. "I'm telling you," he said. "You're going to spoil me. Sit down and have your dinner. You've gone to too much work already, fixing all of this. You shouldn't have done it."

"It is little enough," said Marie-Jeanne, whose household it was, and who was a slender and tall woman with a determined face. "How humble this must seem to you after the richness of America."

"*Bho!*" my father laughed. "You're talking to one whose tablecloth has been a piece of canvas on the ground."

But that made no impression whatsoever. They acted as if they had not even heard him, or if they had, didn't see why that had anything to do with it. Finally, he stood up in exasperation and, grasping each sister by the shoulders, guided them to their chairs and sat them down. "Now, sit and have your dinner in peace," he said amid squeals of laughter from the children, "and I will do the same."

He began to chide his sister, Marie, who was sentimental, and every time she spoke would weep and could not finish what she wanted to say. "If you're going to feel that bad about seeing me," he told her, "I'll begin to wonder why I came. You're acting like it was my funeral."

"Oh, no! Don't think that!" she protested in horror. "It is because I am so happy that I am crying."

"Well, I wouldn't have known it," my father said, and, when the others laughed, reached out and patted her hand and immediately ruined his effort, because she burst into tears again.

"If only Mamma and Papa could be here this day," she cried.

My father nodded thoughtfully. "It would have been something, all right," he said. "I wanted very much to see them once more. And maybe there was a day when I would have come just for that. But, you know, when you wrote that they had given up the tenancy on the old property and had gone to Montory to live, it took the heart out of me. I was still young enough then that I wanted the old home to come back to."

"And how many times have we regretted what they did," said Marie-Jeanne, who had been the nearest to my father in age and so had shared his childhood on the old property. "But they were too old to work hard any more, and we had gone to other properties, and Mamma at least knew that none of you three who went to America would ever come back."

"Maybe I should have," my father said.

"No, you had your own life to live," said Marie-Jeanne. "The money you sent back was happiness enough for them. It gave them a good old age."

When Gabrielle spoke, the table fell quiet, because she was one of the older sisters and demanding of respect. Her face was incredibly lined and she wore the long, black, and high-collared dress of the *amatchi*. But her voice was strong and so like my Uncle Pête's in America had been that it was like a voice out of the grave.

"Mamma knew that you least of all would stay in the old country," she said, pointing a bent finger at my father. "Even when you were a boy and she would see you riding barefoot down the hills on your *makila*, with the grass singing and the wind blowing your black hair, she would say to me, 'Already, he is feeling his wings. This nest will never hold him.'

"And again, that summer when you were only twelve years old, and they sent you to the high Pyrenees to watch the sheep and live in the stone huts and learn to be alone, and you came back at the summer's end with the first look of a man in your eyes, Mamma went to her room and put her arms about her breast and held herself, and cried, 'Now, even my baby has gone from me.' And a little later, when Pierre and Pête went to America, she knew in her heart that you too would go."

As they talked of their childhood on the old property, eyes lined with age grew soft with melancholy, and time slipped away, and for a moment they were young again.

They talked of youthful treks after mushrooms into the deep forests and of their fear of the timber wolves that everyone talked about but no one had seen, of market days when they would sell their chickens or the lambs that they had raised themselves, and how with a little of the money at least they would buy the candy treat they had really gone to all the work for in the first place. They talked of feast days and gay costumes and the singing and the dancing, of childhood loves and heartbreak and tragedy.

They talked of ghosts and haunted houses, and of the time Pête had gone to the high property of Gabrielle and her husband when no one was there, and while he was pitching hay to the oxen noticed that for every forkful he threw someone invisible was throwing another, and how he threw his pitchfork at the shadows and fled through the night, all the long miles down the mountain, and refused ever to go back again.

They talked of the time my father had been smoking behind the barn and of the spanking his mother gave him, and laughed gleefully when he said he never forgot the spanking, and never smoked again either. They talked of the time Pierre had come back from his military service in Africa and filled his brothers with wondrous tales of camels and desert horses and blackskinned people, and how after a taste of that nothing could have kept him in the Basque country. And, finally, they talked of death, of mother and father and the brothers who had remained in the Basque country, and my father in his turn told of the deaths of Pierre and Pête in America.

But when he began to tell a little about their lives, of Pierre's fierce independence and his feuds with the other cattlemen in the plains country where he lived, and of Pête's unmarried and lonely life, first as a buckaroo and then a sheepherder, Marie exclaimed in dismay, "But how little we know of you! How little you have lived here with us after all! And when you speak of America, I look at your face and I can see it. You are our brother and yet a stranger to us."

My father regarded her with the most peculiar expression on his face. But before he could speak, Maurice, who had been quiet throughout much of the meal, rose to his feet and lifted the wine bottle and exclaimed, "Enough of memories for now. Let us have a toast and a *kantu* to the prodigal who has returned!" He filled the wineglasses, and to everyone's merriment toasted him in a booming voice, "To the good health and long life of the old countryman who has come back to his own. But when he looks at our pretty girls, may he please remember his age."

Even while everyone was drinking and laughing at my father's embarrassment, Maurice began a song, grinning at their surprise, because it was a *zhibero* song.

In a moment, all were singing, old and young alike, in the clear-eyed and happy way of people for whom singing is a part of life. And the chorus had an echo, ringing and strong and deep-chested, and for a moment I could not understand what had happened, until I realized that it was coming from the street outside.

But the sisters knew who it was instantly, because they wagged their heads and made patient sighs. Marie Jeanne went to the door and called out, "All right, all right. Come in and see him!"

They were nephews come down from the properties to see their *oita,* and they converged on him in a flurry of berets and sunbrowned faces and shouting salutations. And over the confusion, Maurice's voice boomed out, "Wine! More wine! This is a night for singing!"

A night mist had shrouded the village, and the figure of the gendarme was dark and indistinct beneath the solitary street lamp where he stood. At the sound of our footsteps, he turned inquiringly toward us, but as we approached he drew one hand from beneath the long cloak and touched it to his cap and bade us good evening.

The streets were empty and wet, and the only sounds were our footsteps echoing hollow against the stone buildings. We walked along in silence for a long time, still a little dazed from all the singing at the homecoming dinner. We had gone to the little hotel for rooms, but my father had been unable to sleep, and so we had dressed and gone out for a walk.

Every once in a while, he had paused to look at a darkened store front, and now he said, "Nothing much changes here. Same buildings, same kind of stores, and even the same names on the windows."

"I think I know what you mean," I said. "Everything looks like it's been here a thousand years."

"It's old, all right," he said. "I guess it must be why they call it the old country." He laughed. "Right now, it's beginning to make me feel a little old myself."

"You shouldn't, Pop," I said. "If you don't mind my saying so, I couldn't help thinking tonight how much younger you looked than your sisters."

"I don't know," he said. "It sure made me feel funny to look at them around the table, and I bet it did them too, when the last time we saw each other we was so young. It seems like a man don't pay much attention to the years going by and don't even know what he looks like himself until he sees the face of someone he hasn't seen since he was young. You know," he said, "I wonder if that's what does it, why it makes you suddenly feel your age when you come back to where you was a boy. Like going down this street. I can remember walking along here barefoot and all excited about nothing in particular. And now, I don't have that feeling any more, and it bothers me until I think and get the time straightened around in my head."

We had reached the market place. We stood at its

outer rim and watched the mist settling downward, suffusing the dim street lamps and bathing the cobblestones and the buildings until they glistened with wetness. There was a light moving in a store only a little distance from us, but my father was so engrossed in looking at the market place that he did not seem to notice. The light came to the doorway, and someone stepped outside and pulled the door shut after him. At the sound, my father turned his head to look. The word came out of him like a gasp, "Sauveur!"

At the sound of the name, the man with the light stopped and regarded us curiously, but said nothing. He was a young man with black hair and sharp features.

My father was overcome with embarrassment. "I'm sorry," he faltered in Basque. "I thought you were someone else."

The young man stepped closer and beamed his light at us. His black eyes moved from my father's face to his American suit. "You are Dominique?" he asked. And when my father nodded, the young man said, "I had heard you were coming. My father spoke often of you."

There was a silence, and then my father asked, "He is dead?"

"Yes," the young man said quietly. "Nearly seven years."

"You look very much like him," my father said.

"That is what the people say," the young man answered.

They talked for only a few moments, and then my father excused us, saying, "The time is late. I will come to your store and visit with you again."

129

"*Milesker*," the young man said. "I would like that."

We walked in silence back along the street we had come. My father did not speak until we had almost reached the hotel, and then he said, "What a terrible mistake to make."

I knew what had been on his mind, and I said, "Don't feel that way. It happens to everyone."

He shook his head slowly. "No," he said, "only to the old."

14

The house of Papa Pierre, the cabinetmaker who was the husband of my father's invalided sister, lay on a steep side street in the village of Montory. His workshop was in back, but the scent of new wood and resins and oils lay faintly throughout the house and even reached into the street outside, so that the women passing by on their way to the fountain for water would lift their heads and smell of its fragrance and go on their way with pleased little smiles.

Papa Pierre was a round little man in baggy *pantalons* and a beret that he wore on his head constantly, even through mealtimes. He had a mustache, now gray and straggly, that he had nurtured since military service in his youth. It gave him the appearance of being stern, and he looked as though he might have been when he was younger, but now he was jovial and even a little emotional.

Despite the illness of his wife, the house was a happy

one. It would have been hard to know from talking to Papa Pierre or their son, who was also named Pierre and who was a cabinetmaker too, or his wife and their children in turn, that anything was wrong. I think it was because of the grandmother herself, who seemed to accept adversity as part of life, and once it had happened dismissed it with a shrug of the shoulders and learned to live with it.

Illness had not dampened her authority either. When we first arrived, we were swept up with the welcome, and it was natural that it would take a little time. But we had no sooner entered the house than there was a pounding from upstairs. Madeline, who was the young Pierre's wife, sent one of the children to find out if anything were wrong. He scurried up the stairs, and came back just as quickly. Solemn-faced, he went up to my father and tugged at his sleeve until he had his attention, and said, "You had better go upstairs. She is getting mad at you."

Madeleine, his mother, colored and tried to silence him. "Not really," she said to my father. "She's just excited."

"You don't have to explain," my father grinned. "I know her pretty well." But he excused himself nevertheless and went upstairs. And in a moment the pounding stopped.

I occupied myself for a time coping with Papa Pierre and his cigarettes. When we had first arrived, he had pressed me into taking one, and it was like breathing fire. But from that moment on, he was constantly at my elbow with the cigarette package in his hand, and it was impossible to refuse him. When I would furtively try to slip one of my own cigarettes out of the package in self-defense, he would invariably catch me and offer me another one of his. My head was spinning when little Jean came to my rescue with the message that the grandmother wanted to see me.

Jean led me upstairs to the door, and then went back. When I came in, my father and his sister were holding hands like sweethearts, but there were no tears. She was in an armchair beside the bed, and there was a brightly colored robe over her knees. She resembled my father so much that they could have been twins, from her lean face and gray eyes to the thick, white hair that came down to a widow's peak in front. Her face was pale and thin as porcelain from sickness and long confinement, and hands that once had known hard work now were fragile and weak. She was old and pretty in an embroidered cap and a little shawl that covered her shoulders.

"Come here to me," she beckoned when I paused in the doorway.

I did so, and she leaned forward for my kiss.

"Now, stand near me so that I can see you," she said. Then, having appraised me, she turned to my father.

"America must be good," she said. "He holds his head high. And you, too," she said to him. "Except for the snow up there," and she patted him on top of his head, "the mountain is as proud as when it was young." She turned her attention to me again and sighed, "I cannot yet believe it. How many times have I prayed to Him for this one blessing before I died, to see my Dominique and one of his children of America."

"Don't talk of dying," my father said. "You have many good years in front of you."

"No, no," she said. "You know better than to say that to me. When the end comes, it comes, and words will not stop it. But now, it will be a happier one because I can have told you good-by, my little brother." She put her old hands on his, and for a while she could not speak. But she shook her head quickly, and when she looked at me again her eyes were clear.

"How difficult it is to realize what I am seeing," she said to me. "If I close my eyes, I see your Basque face and I can see you with a beret and with wooden shoes and with a *makila* in your hand. But when I open them, I see a young man who is educated, who is a gentleman in fine clothes. Can you understand how hard it is for me to realize that?" She turned to my father and lifted his hand and squeezed it. "Dominique, Dominique, think of it," she said. "Your children lawyers and teachers and journalists, the first of our family to make their life not with their hands, but with their minds. What a wonderful thing that you could have gone to America!"

After a moment, my father nodded his head. "I never thought about it in that way," he said. "It was their mother who wanted so badly to send them to college. That seemed to be all she wanted in her life, to see them with an education. I couldn't see why at first, and afterward I guess I just took what they were doing for granted. But now, I see what you mean, and," he paused thoughtfully, "what she meant all those years." And then, my father looked up at me as if he had never seen me before.

It was autumn afternoon, and the air was rich with the scents of ripened fields. In the times of silence, there was the drone of insects hurrying to finish their business before end of day. The fern-covered slopes that stretched toward the high Pyrenees were red with color, and in the distance the tall poplars that marked my father's home were tipped with gold.

Once, when the road passed a place of high ground and the property lay before us in full view, my father stopped and tipped back his hat and stood a long moment looking at it. Beyond the stand of poplars, the house loomed with its curving black roof and stone walls that tapered to one end and gave way to the low, sod-covered barn. And beyond that rose green fields where, even now, we could see the handful of sleek brown work cows and shining white sheep grazing together beneath the apple and walnut trees.

Until that moment, my father had been cheerful and talkative on the walk from Tardets. But now, he fell quiet. His head was bent as if he were afraid to look at too much of what was around him, and his steps as we descended from the rise were almost reluctant. His sister, Marie-Jeanne, who had come with us, said nothing but only looked at me with a little closing of her eyes.

Where the road turned off into the dirt path that rose to the property, there was a low, stone fence with moss growing soft over the top and in the cracks, and when we paused there my father leaned with his back against the fence to look at the pasture, and when he did his fingers unconsciously found their way to the cracks and gently rubbed the moss that was there.

An old work cow with long and graceful horns, who had been standing beneath a walnut tree, looked up at our approach and then came slowly down to the fence where my father stood. He took her head in his hands and pulled it back and forth and reached over and smoothed the worn place where the yoke had made its mark, and murmured to her, "*Gaichoa*. If I didn't know better, I would think you were my own old friend."

He took her by the horns and pushed her head back into the pasture, and said to us, "I wonder if we should go to the house after all. I hate to bother the people when they're probably so busy."

"They are expecting us," said Marie-Jeanne. "I sent word that we were coming to visit, so I think that we had better go in."

My father shrugged and led the way up the winding path. The way turned for the last time and we could see through the iron grating of the high gate the house suddenly and intimately before us. But when he put his hands on the gate and began to open it, there was a rusty, creaking sound, and he stopped again, as if listening.

There was a flagstone walk with grass growing through the rocks that led to the front door, and on both sides of the walk there were berry bushes and old, gnarled trees. When we reached the doorstep, Marie-Jeanne went up to knock, but before she could the door opened to frame a young Basque woman and, peering from behind her long skirts, a little girl.

"*Aintzina,*" the woman said with a smile.

The room was big and shadowy, with walls and

floor of stone, and at the far end a fireplace with a cooking pot hanging in it, and above a mantel with brass and copper utensils glinting in the dim light. There was a long wooden table in the middle of the floor, and the young husband of the house was standing beside it, smiling bashfully.

We sat down on the wooden benches while the young wife brought wine and glasses to the table. She looked strangely at my father when he sat down without looking around once, but instead began to talk to the young man. She said nothing until we had finished our wine, and then she said to him, "Can you remember where you slept?"

He nodded and gestured with his head to a room at the side, and then turned away to talk to the husband again. In a little while, she spoke about it again. "Don't you want to see the room?" And then, not waiting for his answer, she took him by the hand. "Come see it."

He went with her then, and through the doorway we could see him looking about. But the only thing he said was, "I remember that crack in the wall, the one almost like a face."

When he came back into the big room, Marie-Jeanne was standing at an old, high-backed wooden bench beside the fireplace. There was a sewing basket on the seat.

"Do you remember this, Dominique?" she asked. "Do you remember Mamma sewing here by the firelight?"

I think he turned before he realized what she was going to say, because his eyes narrowed with pain and a little sound was torn out of him. Then, the mask fell again over his face, and he went to the table and picked up his hat and began to thank the young couple for their hospitality and to tell them that we had to be going. Despite their protests, he said good-by and went to the door to wait for us.

The first twilight came as we were returning to Tardets, and the valley was wrapped with the warm glow of afterday, touching everything with a softness that was almost unreal. But down the path and the long road, never once did my father look back.

15

"You must understand that it was a new country then," my father said. "It was all open land, hundreds of miles of it in that corner of Nevada, and by the law you were free to graze your stock in any part of it."

"But if there were that much free land, which I must confess to you, Uncle, I find hard to realize," said Bernard, a nephew with a property near Montory, "I cannot understand why there was trouble."

"Well, the country's not like here," said my father, raising his hands a little helplessly, "where the land is so rich you don't ever have to worry about enough feed. There, it was nearly all desert land with sagebrush and a few wild grasses, and where the feed and the water were good were the places that the sheepmen and the cattlemen fought about."

It was after dinner, and the conversation was of Jean, the young man who had gone to America with my father. His death had always been a mystery explained only by fragments in letters, and even his parents had died without ever knowing the full story.

"Perhaps I am being stubborn in not seeing what you are trying to say, *Oita,* and if I am, have patience with me," said Bernard. "But with feed and water as scarce as you say, could not the sheep have followed the cattle over the same land?"

"I know what you mean," my father said, "and of course I've seen it happen there many times, sheep making a living over range that cattle have already grazed out. But that can work only where there is much feed to begin with. In the ranges that I am speaking about, there was so little feed that an arrangement like that was impossible. The sheep would have had to travel too far in order to get enough to eat, and they would have ended up poor that way too. So, the sheepmen as well as the cattlemen wanted first chance at whatever feed there was."

"And the water?" said Bernard.

"Well, that's a different matter," said my father. "The cattlemen claimed their stock wouldn't drink in the waterholes and the creeks after sheep had watered there. Some of them said it was because of the oil smell in the wool, and others said it was because the sheep muddied up the water. However," he added with a grin, "I've never known cattle to have too many manners either about what they did around the creeks. The truth of the thing is that if cattle were thirsty, they'd drink in the same creek, all right."

Bernard shrugged. "It has happened here every day for a thousand years." He leaned back in his chair with a smile and said, "It seems to me that perhaps there were many stubborn people in America then."

My father laughed. "Maybe it's true, at that. God knows the government settled the trouble easy enough later on by dividing up the range. But you must also understand that, in America, everybody is touchy about their rights, and it was especially that way among the stockmen in those days, because nearly every one of them had made everything they had out of nothing. And when there was trouble among men like that, they wanted it settled quick, and many times the law had little to do with it."

"Ah! That I can understand," said Bernard. "Sometimes, there are troubles that can only be settled without the law."

"That's true," my father said, "and I think this was one of them. "A man knew for himself what was going on, but proving it was another thing."

"And now of Jean?" urged Bernard.

"Well, as you know," my father said, "when we first went to America, we were separated and we did not see each other often, except for when we both happened to meet in Reno during times off for the year. After one of those long times of not seeing each other, we both found ourselves signed up with this big sheep outfit in the northern deserts. Jean's brother, who as you remember had gone to America first, was a camptender with this outfit. Jean and I started out herding sheep, and then later the boss put me on camptending, because I could handle horses pretty good and broke a lot of them for him too.

"The trouble had started even before we came. There was a big cattle outfit in the same country, and there had been some pretty bad arguments about the range. And then, suddenly, it began to get bad. It got so that when our boss and the boss of the cattle outfit happened to go at the same time to town, which amounted to a few houses and a store and a saloon, and the only town in that whole country up there, the sheriff had to watch them both every minute. But, even then, they finally got into a fight in the saloon, and they had to separate them before they beat each other to death.

"After that, things got rough and every one of us on both outfits suffered a little from it. It seemed like trouble was breaking out all over. I had my own touches of it too.

"I remember once when I was herding and I was camped near a little creek and the sheep were watering there. I'd gone down to the creek above where the sheep were and was washing my clothes and not paying much attention to anything. I didn't even see the two cowboys coming until my dog started barking, and by that time they were between my camp and me. I saw right away that they both had guns on and that they were looking for trouble, and I could have kicked myself for letting them catch me like that, because my carbine was still in the camp.

"There wasn't much I could do about it, though, so I just stood up and waited for them. They stopped their horses but didn't get off, and the argument started right away when one of them said to me, 'Get your camp packed and get those sheep out of this creek.'

"When he said that, it made me mad. 'The hell I will,' I told him. 'You get out and damn quick too, before you catch yourself some misery.'

"The tallest one of them, who was doing the talking, got mad then too, and he said, 'I oughta whip you, you goddam Basco.'

"Well, that did it. When he said that, I went a little out of my head and I made a jump to drag him out of that saddle. And I damn near did it, too, but he jerked the horse around and pulled away a few steps, and when he faced me again he had that gun in his hand. 'I oughta shoot you right now,' he said. 'Now, get moving those sheep or we'll move them for you.'

"By that time, I'd lost my head completely. 'We'll see about that,' I told him, and I started going for the camp where my carbine was leaning up against a tree. He came right after me on that horse, with the other cowboy following, and I knew he was going to shoot me as soon as I got my hands on that gun. Well, God must have given me a little sense right about then, because just before I reached it I stopped and turned around to him and said, 'If you're going to shoot me, you're going to have to shoot me in the back.' And then, I started running toward the next camp, which was just about a mile over the ridge. He must have been mad enough to want to do it anyway, because as I was running I heard the other cowboy shout to him, and then they were both arguing in loud voices.

"Well, the way I felt, it took me only a few minutes to get to the next camp. The herder was asleep and he didn't even know what had happened until I'd taken his carbine and started back to my own camp. When I came over the ridge, I saw that the cowboys were running the sheep out of the creek, so I came down that hill shooting. My shots must have come pretty close,

143

because one of the horses reared up and almost threw his rider. And when that happened, both of them left the country in a hurry. I went back up the ridge and watched, and the last I saw of them they were still going like hell."

Bernard, who had been listening almost with an air of wonder, beat the table gently with his clenched hand. "I can see that America then was no country for a man who wanted to live in peace," he said.

"No, that's not true," my father said, shaking his head firmly. "You would have been surprised at how many didn't want trouble at all, and who would have quit their jobs rather than carry a gun for anything that had to do with fighting.

"Even with as much trouble as there was between the two outfits, and both with orders to wear or carry a gun out on the range, there were herders and there were cowboys who never would. I found a cowboy like that once, and afterward I was always a little bit sorry for what I did to him. But then," he said, throwing up his hands, "everything had gotten so bitter that you punished things you probably would have forgiven any other time.

"It happened when I had been made a camptender, taking supplies to the herders out in the deserts. One day, pretty far from anywhere, I came around the edge of this hill and I saw a cowboy down in a ravine. He had found one of our stray sheep, a yearling, and he had cut its throat and was butchering it for the meat."

My father sighed. "Well, that happened pretty often on the range, herders killing a young beef or cowboys killing for some mutton for a change of diet. And any

144

other time it wouldn't have bothered me that much. But now, of course, it did. As soon as I saw what he was doing, I threw off the tie rope to the pack horse, pulled my carbine out of the scabbard, and started running my horse down the hill.

"The cowboy didn't even wait to pick up his knife. He jumped on his horse and took out of that ravine like a deer, with me right after him. He had a good horse, all right, and when we got up on the flat, he started leaving me a little behind. I was just about to give it up when I saw that instead of cutting away from this canyon in front of us, he was heading right into it. He must have been a cowboy new to that country, because it was a box canyon with no way out.

"After he went in, I knew I had him, and so I slowed up a little and set the hammer back on my carbine. When I came around the last rock, there he was at the end of the canyon, facing me with his horse standing still and nowhere to go. I pulled my horse back to a walk and I kept the gun pointing at him. But when I got closer, I saw that he didn't have a pistol or a rifle or anything with him. He was young and pretty badly scared, because he was white and his lips were shaking. That took some of the mad out of me, and for a minute I almost turned around and left. But then, some of the things that the cowboys had been doing to our herders came back to me. And so, I rode up to him, and when I got alongside I hit him across the side of the head with the carbine. It hurt him a little, I guess, but not much. When I got to the turn in the canyon, I looked back and he was just beginning to sit up on the ground."

My father grinned a little and said, "It's a funny

thing, but many years later I met that cowboy on the street in Reno. We both said hello and kept on going, but I got to thinking afterward it was the first time we'd heard each other talk."

"They say some things have to get worse before they can get better," my father said, "and maybe it's true, at that, because this business got as bad as it could get."

"*Jesu maitia,* I do not see how things could be much worse than what you have told us," said Bernard, doubtfully.

"It was worse, all right," my father said. "But not in any way that you could possibly expect." He laughed shortly, "For that matter, not in any way we expected either."

He spread his hands in front of him, "Now, in all this trouble between the two outfits, there had been some bad arguments and some fights and beatings and even some shooting, but not one man had been killed. There'd been threats and a lot of talking about it, of course, and it could have happened anywhere along the way. But there would have had to be a damn good reason before anybody on either outfit went that far. It's not an easy thing to kill a man, you know."

"Well, anyway," he went on, "all that changed in a hurry. One day, the boss came back from town with a wagonload of supplies. He looked awful worried, and after dinner that night he called all of us into the ranchhouse and told us what he had heard in town. So the story went, the cattle outfit's boss had brought in a dangerous man from Montana to finish the trouble once and for all and run us out of that country. He wasn't sure whether it was the truth or not, because he couldn't believe the cattle boss was the kind of a man to do something like that, actually to hire a man who made a business of killing people. But it was the story, and until we found out different everyone was to be careful.

"We found out damn quick," my father said, "and we didn't have to wait very long to do it. It happened right out in the desert, when one of the herders came back to his camp at night with the sheep. He had fixed his dinner and had pulled a new loaf of bread out of his sack. Whoever did what they did must not have known the custom, because the herder, who was a Basque, scratched the sign of the cross with his knife on the new loaf and cut off the first piece for his dog. The dog ate it, all right, and in less than a minute he was dead.

"The herder walked all the way back to the main ranch that night with the loaf, and when the boss opened it up he found that someone had punched a hole in it and put cyanide in. We didn't need to figure very long to know who had done the trick.

"After that, things changed a lot around the ranch. Where before the men would talk mad about the cattle outfit, now they were pretty quiet about the whole thing. I'm telling you, it's a funny feeling to know that a man like that is free in the country.

"The boss sent the camptenders out to the bands, which were scattered all over the desert, to tell the herders to keep in sight of their camps all the time, and if they couldn't, to pack everything on their burros. And, for Christ's sake, to keep their carbines with them and not trust anybody on a horse.

"Most of them were careful, all right, and did what the boss said. But some of the young herders we had were young from the old country and trusted everyone, or were just too goodhearted to think that anyone would really want to kill them. And that's exactly how what happened next did happen.

"One day, a young herder saw a man on a horse coming across the desert to his camp. The herder got a little worried at first, but the man on horseback didn't seem to be in a hurry about anything, and he even waved from a long ways off. So the herder left his carbine in camp and came out to meet him. The man on horseback had red whiskers and a big belly, and he laughed a lot and acted real friendly when they started talking. In a little while, the herder asked him if he wanted a cup of coffee, and then he turned his back to walk to the camp. That was his mistake. He hadn't gone a dozen steps when the rope snaked him off his feet, and, the next thing he knew, he was being drug behind a running horse over the desert.

"I found that boy the next day when I came to tend camp, and I never want to see a sight like that again. It seemed like all of his skin and half of his hair was gone. I don't know how he managed to live through it, but he did. I rolled him up in a canvas and laid him on the pack horse and took him to the ranch. We did what we could there, and then the boss took him in the wagon to Reno, which was a pretty long trip. But he lived through every bit of it. He must have been awful tough inside.

"That scared the rest of the herders enough not to

take any chances. In fact," my father said, grinning, "it got so they didn't trust anybody on horseback. One day, one of them even took a warning shot at me, and I had to shout like hell in Basque before he would let me get close.

"It didn't stop the badman, though. After he'd been scared off from a few camps, he tried something else. And, this time, it had to be Jean, who as I told you was still herding one of the bands.

"This one night, he had camped out of the wind behind this ridge, and the sheep were bedded down in the flat below him. To show you how much this badman meant business, he must have spotted the camp the day before and then come up in the night to wait for daylight in the rocks on the other side of the ridge. Then, as nearly as we could put it together afterward, he just waited there until Jean walked away from his camp in the morning, probably to look at the sheep before he had his coffee.

"The badman must have come over that ridge at him awful quick, because from the tracks it didn't look as if Jean had even made a move before he was roped.

"This time," my father said, grimly, "it was three days before anyone found him, and then it had to be his brother who did. When St. Martin came to tend camp, he found the sheep scattered for miles in every direction. He ran his horse all the way to the camp, but he couldn't see a thing until he found the tracks of the badman's horse coming down over the ridge. And then, of course, he knew what the buzzards were for, and he followed his brother's blood over the desert and through the rocks until he found him. By that time, there wasn't much left of him.

"The boss and I had been riding out together, and when we came back to the ranch we noticed right away that something was wrong. The cook told us what had happened and where the men had gone. We went into the bunkhouse where Jean's body was, and the boss went to look, but I couldn't do it to save myself.

"We threw our saddles on some fresh horses and left the ranch as fast as we could cover ground. And in the times that we slowed down, the boss begged me to help him talk sense to St. Martin and the men. He kept praying out loud to Jesus and Mary and every saint he knew that the men hadn't done anything foolish yet.

"Well, his prayers must have been answered, but it was a little too close for me. When we came into the cattle ranch that was the headquarters for the outfit, we didn't have to look far for anybody. The cattle boss and the cowboys must have all been working in the corrals when St. Martin and the men jumped them, because they were all together. The herders were lined up inside the fence with their carbines cocked, and the cowboys were gathered in a little bunch in the middle of the corral. But the Montana badman wasn't among them, and we found out later that he'd been in town drinking for days.

"Some of the cowboys must have asked for the chance to make a last prayer, because they were down on their knees with the tears running down their faces, and the others were just standing there looking brave but pretty bad off.

"I don't know how the boss did it," my father sighed,

"because God knows, the way I felt, I wasn't any help at all. But the boss argued and begged and prayed like I never heard a man talk in my life, and finally he convinced St. Martin that it would be murder to kill those men, that they weren't responsible for what happened to Jean, and that all of them would have to go to prison or be hung if they went through with it. When he was finished, the cattle outfit's boss found his voice and swore that he would fire the man from Montana that very day, which he did, and claimed he never knew he was bad, and he almost got himself killed all over again for even saying it. But it all worked somehow, and the boss rounded up part of the men and went back to the ranch. The rest of them said they had business in town."

My father stopped and filled his glass with wine and took a long drink. When he did not go on, Bernard looked at him questioningly and asked, "Was that the end of it?"

"It was the end of the trouble, anyway," my father said evasively. "After that, both outfits just bent over backward to get along on the range. There was never another argument between them all the time I was there."

"But what of the badman of Montana?" asked Bernard, his face still unsettled.

"Well, he headed back for Montana that same night," my father said, again with finality in his voice.

Bernard leaned back in his chair and almost did not ask the last question. But then, something dawned and he leaned forward intently. "If there was an incident, Uncle, I do not want you to tell me who was involved since we may know their people," he asked. "But simply answer me this. Did the badman go back to Montana?"

My father stirred uncomfortably, and then finally, he sighed and said, "No, he only made it to the last street light in town."

Nazario was a wizened little man in Tardets whose greatest claim was that he had been to America. In his youth, he had always been the boy that people made jokes about and never took seriously. So, he had gone away to herd sheep and make his fortune and come back to buy a rich property and acquire a wife and dignity. But he managed only to accomplish part of the dream, that of going to America and herding sheep.

He had worked for seven years and had made more money than he would have in a lifetime in the Basque country. But weakness had followed him there, too, and in his yearly times off to go to town he had managed to spend every penny of it. He would have ended up like so many of the other pitiful little ones, but from somewhere he had summoned enough sense and courage to save some of his wages for the trip back. He came home to the Basque country with nothing but the clothes he wore. His only treasures were his experiences and an American city hat of the vintage of that time, which he put away and cared for as his most precious possession.

So much of his time in America had been spent alone in the hills that he never managed to learn English very well, but just enough to get along. In the first few years of his return, the little knowledge of the language was fresh enough in his mind so that he could still use it. And the rare times in which he was required to do so, when a chance English or wealthy American tourist passing through Tardets needed an interpreter, were tremendous occasions for him.

When he received such a summons at whatever little job he was doing around the village, he would run home and put on the American hat and go to where his special talent was needed. It was often a struggle to make himself understood and to understand, especially Englishmen who spoke with broad accents and used long words, but he managed to do it in spite of his fright at the possibility of failure and disgrace. And this was all that gave him a little bit of prestige in the eyes of the village.

But as the years passed, the language began to slip away from him, until one terrible time when he could not understand what an Englishman wanted. After that, he would not answer any of the summons for his talent, but claimed he was too busy with other things.

It was natural that many of the villagers openly began to question whether he really could speak English after all, especially the younger generation who had never heard him say more than the few, strange cuss words with which he purposely punctuated his speech. In the arguments about it, though, he still maintained he could speak English fluently.

When my father and I first came to Tardets, Nazario did not come to see us, probably because he was being taunted to do so by the young ones who wanted to find out if he knew English. My father, who then was unaware of the dispute about Nazario and the English language, did want to see him, however, because he had known him in his childhood and briefly in America. So, it was arranged that Nazario would be asked to dinner at Marie-Jeanne's. To everyone's surprise, he said he would come, because he wanted to renew his acquaintance with my father, who had been kind to him once in America.

It was then that Marie-Jeanne told us the story about Nazario. When she was finished, her son, Jeannot, asked my father if he would speak to Nazario in English, just to settle the argument once and for all. My father would not hear of it, even when Jeannot said it was not his idea alone, but that of many of the young people who wanted to find out the truth.

"It's not easy to hold on to a language when you don't have a chance to speak it," said my father. "He's probably forgotten it after all these years."

"But why then should he insist that he can still speak the language easily?" said Jeannot.

If my father divined the answer to that, he did not reveal it, but said firmly, "I'm sorry. I'm not going to test him."

"But just a few words is all that we are asking," said Jeannot.

"No," said my father with finality, and Jeannot then

turned to me with his arguments. I told him that, with as much difficulty as I had with French, I had complete sympathy for Nazario and would have no part of it either.

Nazario arrived at dinner in his American hat. It was old-fashioned and it had grown too small for him through the years, so that it seemed to perch on his head, but the felt and the wide ribbon of the band were almost like new. He wore it into the house and until he had shaken our hands in greeting, and then he went back to the hallway and took it off and carefully put it on a hook.

Before the dinner, he was nervous and his thin little face was drawn around the mouth. He began to relax, though, when my father started talking about Nevada and sheep and men they had known together there in common, and it was not long before he was looking from side to side at people in the room to make sure they were listening to these things about people and places he knew in America. By the time we sat down to dinner, he was laughing and slapping his leg and having a great good time.

Jeannot, who had still not given up in his efforts, sat next to me at the long table. As soon as we were seated, he began to nudge me with his elbow to say something in English to Nazario. I whispered no to him as firmly as I could, and he shrugged and gave up the struggle.

Nazario was sitting across from my father at the other end of the table. The soup was served in a large, steaming bowl, and then the bread was passed around. I happened to look up just in time to notice that

Nazario had passed the bread plate on without taking a piece, but paid no particular attention to it. I was the last one to take bread, and so I set the plate down in front of me on the table.

I was raising a spoonful of soup to my lips, when suddenly a voice spoke out in English, with a pause between each word, but nevertheless with a defiant ring, "Robert! Will you please to passing the bread?"

I was so startled that I almost spilled my soup. A hush fell over the table, and everyone looked first at Nazario and then at me. I picked up the bread plate and said as casually as I could, "Okay, Nazario. Here she comes."

The plate was passed to Nazario in silence. He took it with hands that trembled only a little, and then he said to me in the same distinct and defiant voice, in English, "Thank you, Robert, for to passing the bread to me!"

It ended there. My father broke the silence as if nothing unusual had happened by telling Marie-Jeanne about something that had happened that day, and in a moment the table was humming again with conversation. I looked sideways at Jeannot, and he was regarding Nazario with his mouth open, and Nazario was returning the stare with a triumphant expression on his face.

Later that night, when dinner was over, Nazario walked back to the little hotel with my father and me. We talked for a while in French, and then my father switched to English. Nazario was hesitant at first, but in a little while he seemed to break the bonds and speak more freely, and the longer we talked, the easier he spoke. We visited in English for a long time that night outside the hotel, and when he said good night and went down the street, he walked surely and proudly in his American hat.

17

Of the many commissions that my father had been asked to deliver in the Basque country, the silver dollar had the most inauspicious beginning. In fact, when I remembered later how very simply it had all begun, it filled me with wonder.

It had happened on my father's last day with the sheep outfit in the valley near Carson City. A young herder who was a Spanish Basque had asked him if he planned on going down to Pamplona in Spain. My father had answered easily that he thought he probably would. The herder had pondered it for a few minutes, and then went into the bunkhouse to scrawl a few lines on a little piece of wrapping paper, which he tied around a silver dollar he happened to have in his pocket. He gave the tiny parcel to my father and asked him to deliver it to his wife in Pamplona, as a souvenir of Nevada. My father took the parcel and the address, and the herder said thanks and went back to his work.

In our time in the Basque country, the rest of the commissions had not really been too much trouble. In one village, my father had told a cobbler that his brother in America would surely come to visit him the next year. He had told the sister of old Joanes, the herder, in another village that the chances of her brother coming back were slim, but that he was doing fine in America. He had delivered messages and photographs and money and newspaper clippings.

We had seen my mother's birthplace in Baigorry, and we had even spent two nights in a Benedictine monastery where my father wanted to visit with a young monk who had come to talk to him in America. We had been to a dozen villages and sat in many more parlors with stone floors and wooden floors and had drunk good wine. None of it had taken too much time, and there had not been a single complication.

Perhaps if we had made our trip to Spain when we first arrived, the silver dollar would not have been an issue. But once in the Basque country, the distance both to Spain and Pamplona seemed to grow longer each day.

As time went by and the trip to Spain became a probability instead of a certainty, my father took to asking occasionally if the person we happened to be visiting in a certain village went to Spain very often. Everyone said no, and my father shrugged it off and forgot about the commission for the time being.

But later, when the trip to Spain became a doubtful possibility, he began to ask people more frequently if they were planning to go, or knew anybody that was. It was about then that I realized the problem of the silver dollar was beginning to worry him.

Finally, near the end of our stay, the situation suddenly became acute. By then, Maurice had returned in his car to Bordeaux for business, and we were without transportation. My father had lost all desire for a trip to Pamplona, and yet the commission of the silver dollar had to be fulfilled.

My father not only began to ask everyone he met whether they planned to go to Spain, but asked all his nephews in Tardets and the neighboring villages to ask too. We spent entire days walking to the properties of prospective travelers, but, after talking to the people, my father inevitably shook his head and decided to try someone else who would be more certain of going.

And then, one of the nephews came with the message that he had heard of a woman in Mauleon who often went to Spain and would most probably deliver the silver dollar. The only problem was that Mauleon certainly was not within walking distance. However, my father was so desperate by this time that he solved that by ordering the town taxicab for the trip. It seemed to be a perfect if expensive solution, but even this took on complications of its own.

The taxicab driver arrived by appointment early the next morning in his automobile. It had been washed and polished until its old, black surface gleamed, and for the occasion the taxicab driver had put on his best beret and a suit. He had expected to go directly to Mauleon with two and possibly three passengers. But when the elaboration in plans had been explained to him, he was philosophical. It had been decided that, as long as we were going to Mauleon, we should pay a visit to another of my father's nephews in that town. And since we were making the visit, some of the family wanted to go along. Lastly, the house of Papa Pierre in Montory, which was in the opposite direction, had sent word that some of them also wanted to go along, and incidentally to drop off some newly made furniture and linenwork along the way.

The taxicab driver remained calm while the number of passengers grew and even while the bedsteads and the furniture were strapped onto the back and top of his shiny car. He made certain everyone was safely inside and that everything was securely tied down, and then he started the car with great dignity and an impressive roaring of the motor, and we were off to Mauleon. As we rode down the streets of Montory, there was much waving of handkerchiefs and shouting of good-bys.

In direct route, the trip to Mauleon should not have taken us more than an hour even at slow speed. But with the delivering of the furniture and linen at properties and houses along the way, and the visiting and the glasses of wine that went with these stops, it was noon-time when we made our arrival in Mauleon. The taxicab driver, who seemed to be a quiet sort, joined us as we had our lunch and visited with my father's nephew. It was midafternoon by the time we got down to the original purpose of the trip, the business of the silver dollar. And, even then, it was fortunate someone in the car remembered, because, with all the stops and the visiting and the wine and the confusion, both my father and I had completely forgotten about it.

The woman in Mauleon, who lived alone in a little house, was somewhat taken aback at the sudden flood of visitors. However, she was accommodating, and soon we were all crowded into her parlor and having a glass of wine. After a while, my father brought up the commission of the silver dollar and said he understood that she had been to Pamplona.

At this, the woman nodded and beamed with a traveler's pride and said, "Yes, that is right. I have been to Pamplona." She wagged her head and sighed, "How well I remember it." At her answer, my father's face lighted up and he was about to speak. Then she added something, "It will be ten years next month." And with that, she began to reminisce in detail about the trip.

My father's face fell. He waited patiently until she had finished her recollections, and then he made one last effort, although there was little hope in his voice. "Are you planning to go back?"

"Oh, yes," the woman nodded. "I want very much to travel the same road and see once again the sights that I saw, before I die."

My father had been holding the silver dollar in its paper wrapping in his hands. With a heavy sigh, he now put it back in his pocket.

"Would you like me to fulfill the commission when I go?" the woman asked. "I would be pleased to."

"No, that's all right," my father said. "You see, the herder who gave it to me will be coming back to Spain in a year or so, and I would like to get it there before he comes."

"Well, that is a little soon," the woman agreed. "But if you change your mind, let me know."

"I will, I will," my father promised, and, standing up, he thanked the woman for her hospitality.

The trip home passed without incident, except for when we all ate dinner together at the house of Papa Pierre in Montory, and the taxicab driver, who had had a little too much wine, and who by now felt like one of the family, got into an argument with one of my father's nephews at the dinner table. Otherwise, it had been a good day.

About the commission of the silver dollar, my father never did get it delivered. He entrusted it to his nephew, Pierre, who promised to keep looking for someone who might be going to Pamplona. Three years later, my father was still receiving letters to America about it.

ᴐᴎᴐᴎᴐᴎᴐᴎᴐᴎᴐᴎᴐᴎᴐᴎᴐᴎᴐᴎᴐᴎᴐᴎᴐᴎᴐᴎ *18*

Out of the past the memories had come, born in an old album with faded pictures of another time and another way of life in a land thousands of miles away, of dusty men on horseback, of awkward black Cadillacs and men standing together by the fenders in work clothes and suits with high collars, and sheepherders with their burros, and bands of thousands upon thousands of sheep with the sun shining on their backs, and always in the background the gray deserts of our Nevada.

He had forgotten that he had ever sent the pictures or even that there were any of that time. And now, with little sounds of regret and sad shakings of his head, he turned the pages and found scenes and faces of men that called up the years of bigness. Then, midway down one page, the pictures stopped and there were no more, because it was the beginning of sadness and silence.

"That was the last picture and the last letter," said

Marie-Jeanne. "After that, there was nothing for two long years."

"A long time went by before I could bring myself to think about anything but the work I was doing," my father said.

He turned back to a picture of a smiling and dignified man in a suit standing beside him in the dirt. "A lot of people claimed it was the bankers who caused it all, coming out to the sheep camps in their big cars and high-toned talk about lending us as much money as we wanted," my father said, "and maybe they were part to blame at that. But it was our own fault, too. We'd worked hard to get the sheep we had. Every one of us had started out herding when we came from the old country, and we'd saved our money and learned the language and the business ways in America, and we owned the sheep we had without owing anyone.

"But, with money so easy to borrow from the banks, everybody was mortgaging to buy up more sheep and ranches and good land, just to get big. And so we did it, too. Three of us threw in all our sheep together and made a partnership, and then we borrowed money to buy up triple the sheep we had and a rich home ranch to operate from.

"And what an outfit it was," he said, with still a little amazement in his voice. "We ran nearly twenty thousand head of sheep and a few thousand cattle, and we owned wonderful grazing land for fifty miles. We had dozens of herders and buckaroos and so many saddle horses that we never could have used them all. We brought in our supplies by the truckloads, and we even had a store on the ranch where the workingmen could

166

check out anything they wanted against their wages, things like levis and work shirts and jumpers and gloves and tobacco.

"We owned Cadillacs, and when we went to Reno we rented rooms and apartments, and we ate with bankers, and in the saloons we treated the house every time we had a drink." He shook his head. "Sometimes, thinking back, I can't hardly believe it. It was a time like I'd never seen in America before, and never saw again.

"And then," he said, nodding heavily, "the market began to go. At first, everyone said it was just a little slump, and that it would be over with in a hurry. But it wasn't just a slump. It was the end. Before you could even turn around, sheep and cattle weren't worth anything, and you couldn't have sold if you wanted to, because nobody would buy any."

He put his hands to his eyes. "It was the saddest thing to see," he said. "We couldn't even make the interest payments on the mortgages, much less the principal. And then, the bankers started coming out to the camps and the ranches again, but this time they didn't smile very much. First, they began to take the grazing land and the stock, and then they took the ranch itself. They wouldn't even let me keep my beautiful black stallion horse that I had broken and raised myself and that nobody else had ever ridden, and it did my heart good afterward when I found out that the first time they tried to ride him he threw the rider and the saddle and everything and ran away wild to the hills he came from.

"When it was all over, all that my partners and I could keep was one band of a few thousand sheep.

There was even a mortgage on them, but we were paid up clear enough to at least make a new start with them, which was pretty good at that when you think that nearly every outfit lost everything they had.

"The only thing left to do was trail the sheep all the way back up to the northern deserts and the open range where we'd begun. But bad luck was still coming at us. The day before we were to go, the pneumonia hit me and I went down into bed. We were supposed to be off the ranch that next day, because the people who owned it before were coming back, but I was too sick to be moved anywhere, and the doctor from town said I would die if I was. So my wife and I stayed on in the house, and to make up for our lodging and the little food we ate she cooked for the owners.

"I finally got well, but it was days before I even had the strength to walk on my feet. And when I could, and walked around the ranch for a little exercise, all I could remember was the corrals and the fields filled with sheep and cattle and horses and busy workingmen, and the smell of dinner and the sound of the bell from the cookhouse, and smoke from the bunkhouses. And now, the corrals and the fields and the cookhouse and the bunkhouses were empty, and there wasn't a sound anywhere in the world. It was like going to a graveyard, and it almost killed me."

He was silent for a moment. "They say a human being can only take so much of one kind of pain, and then it doesn't bother him very much at that," he said. "But I wonder. Maybe it was because I was well again and winter was over and things would be growing, and the ewes we had in the north would be lambing already, but I began to feel some hope again.

"My wife and I packed up the things we had and went on the stage to Reno, where we found a room for her to stay in while I went north to join my partners. She said good-by to me at the stage. I was still awfully weak, and the weather had suddenly turned bitter cold, but I had a big bearskin coat to keep me warm on the trip.

"That night, the temperature began to go down and down and down. It was the coldest night I ever remembered in my life, and, even being in that big coat and in the stage, I thought I was going to freeze to death. When we got to the stopping place and I stepped outside into the air, my face felt like the skin had frozen, and it hurt you even to open your mouth to talk.

"My partners didn't know I was coming, so all I could do was start to walk the ten miles to where the cabin was. I guess I knew what was coming, all right, but I just couldn't make myself think about it.

"It was a moonlight night and I could see where the cabin with the light in it was from a long ways away. The sheep had been lambing in the flat below, and the road I was walking went right through the middle of them. The sagebrush was covered with frost so that you could see even the tiny branches fuzzed with white. In the moonlight, the sheep were like statues, some lying down with their new lambs beside them on the frozen ground, curled up in the hollow between their mother's legs, and the others standing up next to the brush. They covered the whole flat as far as I could see.

The only sound was my own breathing. They were all dead."

The hillside where my father and I were sitting was sunny and warm. Below us down the soft, green slopes stretched the river, its ripples gleaming white, and the village of Tardets ageless and tranquil in the autumn afternoon. The high peaks of the Pyrenees looked down calmly on the peaceful little valley, as they had done forever before. Far below and to the right of us, there was a property enclosed in its tight little barrier of hedgerows and trees, and there was the tiny figure of a man moving slowly through the fields, as his father and fathers before had done for a thousand years.

From the hillside, my father looked down and watched his progress from squinting eyes in a face where a hundred cruel winds and suns of desert and mountain in another land across the sea had cut a hundred creases.

When he spoke out of silence, it was in the tongue of that land and about that land, and it was to say, "That's going to be some Admission Day parade this year. A fellow in Carson City was telling me they're going to have more hosses in it this year than they ever had before."

"That's what I heard too," I said. "And I guess they're going to have a lot of Indians in it this year. Why were you wondering?"

"Well, you know how much I like that parade. And after all, it's the state's birthday," he said. He took a breath and added, "What I mean is that I think it's about time we went home."

The time for good-by had come, and it was as if they
had never really thought about it until that moment.
The realization seemed to break over everyone at once,
so that they looked at him with eyes suddenly widening
with pain and the knowledge that they would never
see him again, that this was the last good-by. It was a
brooding presence that hung over every last walk down
a familiar lane and every final visit and every dinner
table and every last glass of wine.

It was innocence and fright in the eyes of the children
with whom he had played like a child, because they
knew that when they kissed him good-by it had something to do with death, but they could not understand
because they could not yet understand death.

It was in the sober faces of his nephews and the tears
of his nieces, who bravely talked of impossible trips to
America to see him, but who said the word "Uncle" as
if they were cherishing it on their lips, because they

knew they would never speak it again.

It was heartbreak in the eyes of his sister, Marie, who had never married and who now had found some-one to hold onto for strength and as suddenly lost him, the last of her brothers. "What am I to do without you, my brother, my brother?" she cried. And he said, "Don't cry, please don't cry. I will write to you often."

And she bitterly protesting, "But a cold letter. How can that fill my empty heart?"

It was courage in the eyes of Marie-Jeanne, who smiled and laughed, but with a tremulous whimper in the heart of it, who insisted that with all the miracles of America he would be back again before they had even begun to miss him.

And it was thankfulness in the calm, gray eyes of his dying sister, whom he held as tenderly as a child and promised her long life yet to come, but who shook her head and said, "If God is kind, the next time I see you will be in Heaven."

It was something else in the good-by of his sister, Gabrielle, and her family at the lonely mountain prop-erty high in the Pyrenees.

We had begun our walking trek to the high mountain property in the early morning of our last day in the Basque country. There were no roads into this region, and through the morning hours we mounted steadily higher on old footpaths and trails cut deep into the wet, black earth by generations of men and oxen and sheep.

The paths led through forests of deep shade where the tangled branches formed an arch overhead, through fields so sheer that you could stand erect and reach out with your hand to touch the hillside, and through age-old apertures in the stone fences and thick hedgerows. At times when we crossed over a ridge to begin the climb on another slope, we could catch glimpses through the high berry bushes of the valley below, with the properties in tiny squares and the river a thin, silver vein in the sunlight. And though he had last made this trek as a boy, there was not a trail or a turning in the path that my father had forgotten.

The sun was high overhead and already beginning to tip when he paused in a trail and threw back his head and called. And in a moment, the call was answered from far above, in a lost and distant blast of sound that cupped and echoed down the mountains and whispered mournfully away.

The children came first to meet us, running barefoot like wild forest sprites down the trail, and then stopping a distance away and refusing to come nearer, but still leading the way to the property, where even now we could see the family awaiting us.

The old stone home rested on a ridge with its back against the mountain, and on both sides the ground sheered steeply away. Though there were other properties hidden somewhere below, it was the only house that we could see, and because of this it seemed lonely and forsaken, and I could understand how the legends of its being haunted by spirits had grown.

Young Joseph, the son-in-law of Gabrielle and her husband, and the one who had answered my father's call, came striding down the trail to greet us. He was a lean man with a deep chest and sinewy arms, with a black beret and *pantalons* held up with a rope around his waist, and heavy wooden shoes. Though it was the first time we had seen him, he embraced my father fiercely and then pummeled him as if he had known him forever.

"I had heard people in America had no use for their legs any more," he said. "But you have not forgotten, have you? Tell me, did you find the walking hard?"

"A little steeper than I remembered," my father said. He pointed to the boots that he had brought from America. "But don't fool yourself. A pair of boots like this would last me a lifetime here, but no more than a few months in the mountains of Nevada."

Joseph laughed with strong good humor. "And these?" he said, pointing to his own wooden shoes.

"Yes, and those," my father grinned. "The desert sun would have them on fire in damned few minutes."

Joseph laughed boisterously, and, with his arm around my father's shoulders, led us the last few steps up the trail to where the family was waiting. Gabrielle was there in her long, black dress with the high collar, and her husband, who was called Papa Joseph, had put on a new beret and a black vest for the occasion. The daughters, one of whom was the wife of Joseph, had combed their hair neatly and scrubbed their faces until they shone.

Although it was midday, the main room of the house was thick with darkness, and the only light was from the fireplace, where the cooking was being done in a great, black kettle. When Gabrielle bent over the fire to stir the kettle, and the light danced in reflection from

her old, lined face, it was like a glimpse out of a thousand years of ancience.

The room where we had our farewell dinner was long
and narrow, with the sunlight slanting through tiny
windows in the stone walls. We sat on long, wooden
benches, and my father was in the place of honor at the
head of the table. And the table was heaped with every
treat that they had been able to prepare. It was a feast
that lasted for hours.

There had been singing almost from the beginning
of the meal. At first, there were gay and happy songs,
but as the meal drew toward its end, they were songs
of sadness and mountain airs of melancholy, sung without words.

But it began, I think, when Joseph turned to my
father and said, "At what hour will you leave tomorrow?"

"Very early," my father said. "Probably with the
sun."

Joseph put his hand on my father's shoulder. "Then
know this," he said. "With the first sun of the morning,
I will sing my farewell to you from the mountain up
there."

My father looked at him and then looked away. In a
moment, he stood up and said, "It's a long way down
the mountains, and it will already be night when we
reach home. I think we had better be going now."

For a moment, they protested loudly. But when they
saw that he was determined, they stood up too for the
good-by. And then, the frenzy began. In an instant, they
all were embracing us, shouting and crying and singing at the same moment. As my father went to each of

them, they thronged about him, holding to his arms until the final good-by with Gabrielle, and through the tumult came the voice of Papa Joseph, chanting over and over in the same refrain, "He has gone to America and he has made his fortune!"

When, finally, we had made our way out of the house and were descending the steep trail, with the song of good-by following down after us, someone began to call, "Come back! Come back!"

I looked at my father, but he did not seem even to have heard. His face was white and grim and violently disturbed, and he was breathing in quick gasps. I reached out and touched him on the arm and said uncertainly, "They want us to come back."

Without turning, he shook his head and cried shakenly, "I can't go back. It ain't my country any more. I've lived too much in America ever to go back." And then, angrily, "Don't you know that?"

And suddenly before me, I saw the West rising up at dawn with an awesome vastness of deserts and mighty mountain ranges. I saw a band of sheep wending their way down a lonely mountain ravine of sagebrush and pine, and I smelled their dust and heard their muted bleating and the lovely tinkle of their bells. I saw a man in crude garb with a walking stick following after with his dog, and once he paused to mark the way of the land. Then I saw a cragged face that that land had filled with hope and torn with pain, had changed from young to old, and in the end had claimed. And then, I did know it.

We walked in silence down the wooded trail, and in a little while the voices died away.

176